NOT MADE BY HANDS

IMPRIMATUR:
✠ Most Rev. Sean P. O'Malley, OFM Cap.
  Bishop of Fall River, Mass., USA
  October 15, 1998, St. Theresa of Avila

— *Second Printing, May ,1999* —

OUR COVER: *The two most famous portaits of the two most famous people who walked this earth close to two thousand years ago — the Mother of God and the Son of God. Both are miraculous images, unexplainable by modern science yet authenticated by the careful research of numerous scientists. The author, Bro.Thomas Mary Sennott, draws from his own scientific background in exploring the pros and cons regarding their authenticity.*

ACHEIROPOETA:

NOT MADE BY HANDS

by

Thomas Mary Sennott

The Miraculous Images
of Our Lady of Guadalupe
and the Shroud of Turin

Franciscan Friars of the Immaculate
Our Lady's Chapel, New Bedford, MA
© Copyright 1998

4

Introduction

by Peter Mary Fehlner, F.F.I.

From the very beginnings of the Church it has been a practice cherished by her members to preserve and treasure *mementoes*, souvenirs, relics of the saints, especially of the martyrs, in a word anything which might serve as a record and reminder of those heroes of the faith who confessed their Savior before men in life and in death, what they had done and where they had done it. Whatever they might be, those relics and souvenirs functioned as instruments for the continued presence of those with whom they were once associated and thus shared in the veneration reserved by the faithful for the Saints. In a special way is this true of the holy icons, as it were the very faces of the holy ones.

All Catholics know that the veneration given to the Saints is but an aspect of the honor they give to their God and Savior. In honoring those whom God Himself has honored, greater praise is rendered the Creator who has done such great things in creating and still greater in saving His creation. Relics and icons which are the vehicles as it were of a presence and thus also of that praise for the one made present ultimately point to the Savior Himself who in taking flesh of the Virgin Mary made it possible to have a souvenir of God, to make and venerate His portrait, without committing idolatry. A part of the wonder of the Incarnation is that we can admire in so human a fashion the face of our God.

This is indeed an evident satisfaction of the human heart. But this devotional form has a more particular source in a historical fact: the practice of the Mother of God who kept all those things said about her Child in her heart, pondering them (cf. Luke 2:19, 51). The honor Christians pay to the images of the Savior is but an extension and continuation of the honor and praise and prayer of Mary directed to her Son and Savior. They are a reminder of Him who is the Son of the living God, the Christ, who died on the cross for our sins and rose for our justification (cf. Mt 16, 16; Rom. 4, 25), the Holy One of God who alone has the words of everlasting life (cf. Jn. 6, 69-70). And in this praise of her Savior from the Church and Christians the icons of the Virgin of Virgins - and subordinate to hers those of the martyrs and saints - serve effectively to stimulate and structure in believers that attitude of praise and adoration so perfectly exemplified originally in Mary.

Veneration, then of the relics of the Saints, especially of their holy icons, is a characteristic feature of Catholic piety since the foundation of the Church by its Savior, because it is a tangible,

An Icon of Mary, Mother of God and her Divine Son with John the Baptist and Eastern Doctors of the Church, from Holy Annunciation Convent, Inoussal, Greece

evident confession of faith in the truth of the Incarnation, because it is a connatural way of identifying in daily life with the sacred humanity of God, above all in the most blessed Sacrament of the altar, where the very physical, corporal, carnal reality of what is recalled is really, truly, substantially present. That piety, moreover, is exquisitely Marian at every point, for such devotion and prayer is but the extension and continuation of Mary's for her Child and Savior, the only kind of devotion pleasing and acceptable to God. The words of the hymn: *Corpus verum corpus natum de Maria Virgine* (Body true, body born of the Virgin Mary) well synthesize the depth of that mystery, proclaimed and accomplished at the Annunciation and consumated when Christ was exalted on the cross to draw all men to Himself (cf. Jn. 12, 32).

Since the first days of the Church, indeed from the very public ministry of our Lord, one of the most effective ways of denying the truth of the Incarnation and of the Blessed Eucharist, in practice as well as in theory, for the uneducated and sophisticated alike, has been to show disrespect to the face and image of our Lord and to refuse to honor the relics and icons of the Saints, above all of the great Mother of God. A secular age, inclined to accept without question the assumptions of the rationalist, or to reduce piety simply to a question of emotional balance or pietism, will always prejudge the insistence of the Church on the obligatory character of veneration and devotion to the holy icons as misplaced and obscurantist, infantile, if not downright superstitious. As soon, however, as one appreciates the essential implications of the Incarnation and of the Eucharist in the Church, it is clear that what seemed merely a secondary point of discipline touches in fact the very heart of Catholic life.

In the name of pure monotheism the Pharisees and many of the Jews refused to adore the face of the living God, refused to acknowledge the virginal maternity of His Mother Mary. Subsequently, under Muslim influences and in an attempt to win favor with the Muslim peoples the eastern Roman emperors at Constantinople during the 8th century supported and promoted what is known as the iconoclast heresy, a movement aiming at the elimination and destruction of all the holy images or icons of our Lord and His blessed Mother in the

Churches and monasteries of the Empire. The movement was eventually overcome like all heresy and impiety, but not before an enormous wealth of Christian art had been lost forever. Significantly, eastern Christians regard the condemnation of iconoclasm in the second Council of Nicaea (787) as the triumph of orthodoxy, i.e. of true belief in the divinity of Mary's Child and in the glory of the cross. We may add, if veneration of the holy icons is the characteristic feature of true piety, the triumph of orthodoxy is also that of true piety and devotion over impiety and wickedness.

Throughout the middle ages in the west, especially after the time of Berengarius who first expressly denied the real presence of Christ in the Eucharist, heretics and heretical movements were characterized by iconoclastic tendencies, more or less explicit, never however absent. This was also the case with the Protestant Reformation from its start, nowhere more so than among those English groups commonly referred to as puritanical. In the name of sanctity churches, statues, icons, crucifixes, stained glass windows were violently dishonored and destroyed. One needs only visit a typical New England style church to understand why puritanism is in practice another name for iconoclasm, and what at root is wrong with this kind of theology and spirituality. It is the same thing wrong with the early docetism, it is a denial that the Incarnation makes any difference in the created world, that the body assumed by the Word is a real body and by that fact a sacred body, the body of God. One need only reread the first letter of John with this in mind to realize why docetism and iconoclasm are forms of infidelity, the perennial expression of the rationalist spirit in things intellectual, and of the impure in morals, all that dishonors the human body formed by the Creator to be the temple of the Holy Spirit.

Today the iconoclastic spirit, the rationalist temper has systematically pervaded culture via a glorification of "Science" and technology. A particular manner of studying the material creation and adapting it for human use and comfort, in itself legitimate, has come to be taken as normative for every use of the human mind and as grounds for repudiating the divine, the miraculous the supernatural as outmoded forms of subjective piety, without any objective basis. It is a bias which has led innumerable exegetes, Catholic as well as non-Catholic, to doubt the historicity of the infancy narratives because these record various physical phenomena, above all the virginal conception and birth of the Savior, reputed to be impossible scientifically speaking, and therefore simply impossible. So too, such a mental attitude naturally disposes one to deny that miracles, especially the so-called physical miracles of our Lord's public ministry, involve anything real at the tangible, corporal level, for example, the miracles of changing water into wine, of multiplying loaves and fishes, of walking on the water and calming the sea, of raising the dead, and above all of dying at an appointed hour (and not before) and then at the appointed hour rising to glory on one's own terms, and not those of one's revilers.

This attitude, best described not as scientific, but simply as "scientism," an exaggerated confidence in one's native powers to know and understand the objects of our senses, such that one categorically denies these humble beings either to be real or to be real primarily to proclaim the existence and majesty of the Creator (cf. Rom. 1, 18-20), is no where so obviously and directly opposed to faith than where it directly denies the value and necessity of venerating the holy images of Christ and His Blessed Mother, of prostrating in adoration before the physical reality of the Body and Blood of Christ under the species of bread and wine.

Hence the interest in and importance of two unique icons of the Savior and of the Immaculate Virgin: the Shroud of Turin and the cloak of Bl. Juan Diego, the visionary of Guadalupe in Mexico, with the Virgin's image miraculously imprinted and miraculously preserved incorrupt upon it since 1531. Both as to their content and as to their origin these icons are extraordinary. But whereas the content of every icon may rightly be regarded as extraordinary, the non-believer may often say that only those of artistic value have interest for him. In the value of these two icons, it is not possible to measure the value of image in terms of its human origin, because these two icons have no human author. From their origin they have been recognized by the faithful as "not made by human hands", acheiropoeta, a belief confirmed by serious scientific analysis over a long period of time.

Influential circles have recently attempted to interpret the Carbon 14 dating tests performed on the Shroud of Turin as proof that the Shroud is a pious medieval forgery. Similar attempts have also been made to discredit the Tilma of Bl. Juan Diego. Bro. Thomas in his exhaustive review of these questions enables us to understand why such claims are not scientific, but rather the reaction of iconoclastic scientism in the face of a challenge, a powerful challenge, an irrefutable challenge to the false assumptions of this mentality, and therefore as St. Maximilian observed (SK 1192) an effective demonstration of the credibility of our Savior and of the mystery of the cross. Beholding these two icons one is as it were face to face with the miracle of the Incarnation. Face to face with the Passion of the Crucified and with the compassion of His beloved Mother, it is next to impossible to remain perfectly neutral. One may of course persist in one's iconoclasm, but neither reason, nor that particular domain of reason called natural science, will support the vaunted credibility of the iconoclasts. All the tests, even the inconclusive Carbon 14 test, render homage in their own way to the reality of the image on the Shroud and on the Tilma.

Naturally, if one cannot in the name of science justify scientism in respect to the Shroud and Tilma, then it is no longer possible to approach these merely out of aesthetic curiosity. And while Bro. Thomas is primarily concerned with questions of credibility and apologetics in his study, his conclusions clearly invite the reader to go further, to accept the miracle of the icon "not made by human hands" as a divinely appointed sign, providentially reserved and preserved for a time particularly subject to intellectual deceits of the prince of this world in the form of scientism. To take that step further is to believe in the Son of Mary, and to believe in Him with her help and according to her example.

From a historical and scientific point of view one might have expected first a review of the Shroud and then of the icon of Guadalupe. In fact Bro. Thomas has arranged his exposition in exactly the contrary order, because the study of true icons of the Savior and of His Holy Mother will always reflect the precise character of Catholic piety: Marian because thus directed efficaciously to the Christ, the Son of the living God, the Holy One who alone has the words of everlasting life (cf. Jn. 6, 68-70).

That this is the case is but the most perfect realization of a general principle governing the whole of God's creation. Every creature, from the least perfect to the highest shares a single primary purpose: to signal the existence of the Creator, to reflect in its being His perfections and by its activity to serve and glorify His goodness and wisdom. The harmony of creation is secured precisely in so far as the less perfect realize their end and in sustaining the more perfect in the praise of God. In past ages this structure of the universe was described as hierarchical. Whatever the name, the fact of this order helps us to grasp why the praise of God's goodness and love should be mediated by the most perfect of His works, the Incarnate Word, and why of all His other servants the Immaculate Virgin most thoroughly and effectively brings us to Christ, our Savior, the Son of God.

This reflection is not merely theoretical, it is one immediately pertinent to the actual condition of the universe, infected by sin. It was the sin of the angels, and then the original sin of Adam and Eve which not only disrupted the initial plan of God for His creation, but bid fair to frustrate completely the attainment of that perfect glory intended by God in the Incarnation. The prevision of the Immaculate in virtue of the merits of her Son and Savior free of all stain of original sin from the first moment of her conception, in a way of speaking made it possible for God to risk prudently the sin of our first parents. No sin of theirs could definitively impede the divine plan; it would only affect its mode. The Savior God would be born in poverty and humility and end His life on a cross, and a sword His Mother's heart would pierce to reveal the thoughts of many hearts (cf. Lk. 2, 34, 35).

Many scholars hold that the image of the Virgin on the cloak of Bl. Juan Diego is that of the Immaculate Conception, of the Woman of Genesis who crushes the head of the deceitful Serpent, of the Woman of the Apocalypse who triumphs over the same liar in the form of a great Dragon, the Woman-Virgin espoused to a man named Joseph addressed by the Angel Gabriel by that new name: Full of grace, or as our Lady said at Lourdes, Immaculate Conception. In the words of the Ven. John Duns Scotus, she is qua Immaculate the most perfect fruit of a most perfect redemption by a most perfect Redeemer. Being the primary fruit of His Passion, she is the connecting link between Him and the rest of His brethren and between them and Him, in a word Mediatrix. Her mediation is essentially that of a mother, of the universal catholic Mother, the New Eve, Mother of all the living. Whoever grasps and accepts the credibility of the Immaculate will quickly go on to grasp and accept the credibility of the Crucified and of His Passion, of which she is the most perfect fruit. Just because she is sinless, the directions she gives as at Cana are always effective and miraculous. Is it not a fact that the apparition and miracle of Guadalupe effectively stimulated the evangelization of the Americas and quickly accomplished their conversion to the cross of Christ and entrance into the one true Church.

Recognition and reverence for the image of the Immaculate on the cloak of Bl. Juan Diego will bring us to adore and love the face of Him who gave His life that we might be saved from eternal damnation for eternal life. The mystery of the Immaculate Mediatrix of all grace will lead us to the mystery of our salvation through the Passion of her Son, visually preserved in the image of the Shroud, the reality veiled for us under the sacred species of the Eucharist.

The Militia of the Immaculate founded by the great Franciscan martyr, St. Maximilian Kolbe, exists for one reason only: to promote the spread, everywhere, and adoption by everyone, of a spirituality whose essential focus is the Crucified Savior and His Immaculate Mother, so graphically identified in these two great icons. The controversy surrounding them is but an aspect of that larger conflict between the pious faithful and the scoffing iconoclast which has been present since the founding of the Church. These two icons are a sure sign of the credibility of the Church's position and a warrant of final victory for those on the side of belief, indeed for the possibility of saving present scoffers, of converting them to the One depicted on the Shroud through the mediation of the Immaculate.

Our Lady's Chapel,
New Bedford, Massachusetts.

PART I

The Miraculous Image
of Our Lady of Guadalupe

I am Mary of omnipotent God

the humble Mother, Virgin sovereign

A torch whose eternal light

is the splendid North Star of mankind's hope:

Let a perfumed altar in a holy temple

be installed for me in Mexico,

once Pluto's profane dwelling,

whose horrors

my foot dispels in a storm of flowers.

Sigüenza y Góngora[1]

She said: "Juanito, the smallest of my children, where are you going?" He answered: "My Lady and my Child, I must go to your house in México Tlatilolco to continue the study of the divine mysteries taught us by your priests who are the emissaries of Our Lord." She then spoke and revealed her holy and benevolent desire, saying: "Be it known and understood by you, the smallest of my children, that I am ever Virgin Holy Mary, Mother of the true God from whom all life has come, of the Creator, close to whom is everything, the Lord of heaven and earth. I ardently desire that a temple be built for me here, where I can show and offer all my love, compassion, help and protection, for I am your merciful mother. Here I wish to hear and help you, and all those who dwell in this land and all those others who love me, and invoke and place their confidence in me; and to hear your complaints and remedy all your sorrows, hardships, and suffering."

"And in order to carry out what my mercy seeks, you must go to the bishop's palace in México and tell him that I sent you to make it clear how very much I desire that he build a temple for me here on this place; you shall tell him exactly all you have seen and marveled at, and what you have heard."

Our Lady of Guadalupe to Blessed Juan Diego

Contents of First Part

The Mythology of the Aztec Indians

"Mythology...is reason's attempt to give plausibility to the object of religious belief. Where the believer cannot find - as the Christian can and does find - preambles for his faith in reason and history, he seeks them instinctively in the caricature of reason and history furnished by the mythological story."[2]

The Aztec myths are extremely convoluted and probably will never be completely reconstructed, so thoroughly were they destroyed by the Conquistadors, but at least the broad outlines are clear. The Aztec religion was primarily an astral mythology with gods of the sun, the moon and the stars. On the top of the great pyramid in Mexico City were two chapels containing images of two of the main gods, Huitzlipochtli, the sun god, god of light and of life, and Tetzalipoca, the moon god, god of darkness of death and of hell. The Aztecs believed that every day the sun was conquered by the moon, every day the sun died, and that was why the sky turned red at sunset, from the spilled blood of the sun. But the sun could be brought back to life, rejuvenated by drinking human blood. Huitzilopochtli was usually pictured with his tongue hanging out, thirsting for human blood. In this diabolic twist, it is not God that saves man, but man that saves the god. Bro. Herbert Leies, S.M. writes:

"The gods needed human blood as vital sustenance, the Aztecs argued; otherwise the gods would perish. Without it the sun-god could not run his daily course; without it, the corn-god would not ripen the ears of corn to feed the people. The Aztecs made a compact with their gods, the Aztecs to provide human blood and the gods in turn to furnish the blessings of life. Failure by either would mean destruction.

"Human sacrifices became an obsession with the Aztecs. Blood, the mysterious fluid of life - red, warm, and gushing from the torn-out heart of the victim - was smeared upon the mouths of the idols, and the heart was then offered as a burnt offering to the hungry gods. At times, this became a frenzy in wholesale sacrifice, as at the dedication of the great pyramid temple in 1487, during the time of Emperor Ahuitzotl. Chroniclers give an estimate of 20,000 to 80,000 persons sacrificed on that occasion. A Domnican Friar, Duran, describes the bloody ceremony to the war-god. Prisoners of war were taken from their cages to form long lines that led to the four gates of the great temple compound. Waiting at the gates to dispatch the victims were the kings of Mexico, of Texoco and of Tacuba, and an old priest named Hacacllel, all four decked in their finest costumes, bejeweled and wearing the insignia of their office. For four days, from sunup to sundown, the wholesale slaughter continued at the hands of kings and priest. Skulls by the thousands were added to the great skull-rack next to the sacred ball court.

"On regular feast days of the gods, the ceremony of sacrifice would take place at the top of the temple stairs, where the sacrificial altar stone was in full view of the people. The presiding priest, armed with an obsidian knife, cut out the heart of the victim stretched over the altar stone, to offer it still throbbing to the idol. He then severed the head which would be added to the skull-rack. The headless body would then be tumbled down the temple steps to be given to the Aztec warrior who had captured the victim, or would be shared and eaten by those who assisted at the sacrifice. Those eating the flesh of the consecrated victims believed they would absorb the strength and spiritual powers of the one sacrificed. In their mind, it was not a cannibalistic orgy but a species of communion."[3]

During this dedication in 1487 just six miles from the great pyramid of Huitzilopochtli and Tetzcatlipoca, there lived a thirteen year old boy named Cuauhtlatohuac, "he who talks like an eagle." In 1523 when he was 48 years old in a church built on the very ruins of the great pyramid, "he who talks like an eagle" was baptized, Juan Diego.

At a hill called Tepeyac, just outside the Aztec capital, was another important god, the mother goddess, goddess of the earth, called Tonantzin, which means "mother of the gods" and "our mother." She was also called Cihuacoatl "wife of the serpent." This goddess demanded the blood of women. The Conquistadors destroyed most of these idols, much to the outrage of today's secular humanist Establishment, but in 1790 a colossal statue of Cihuacoatl or Coatlicue was discovered in Mexico which is now kept in the Anthropological Museum. Bro. Bruno Bonnet-Eymard writes:

> "The sight of this monster made one shudder with horror...It is a woman with a jaguar's paws and eagles claws for feet. She has just been beheaded as were all the women sacrificed during the fertility rites; two streams of blood spurt from the severed neck and meet in the form of two confronting serpent's heads, thereby making a strange and terrible kind of human mask...From waist to knees she wears a skirt of intertwined snakes - her chest is covered with a breastplate made of alternate heads and hands, with a skull pendant...Among all the works of the world's statuary, none can compare with Coatlicue for the impression of horror it gives and inspires."[4]

The Aztec religion is the cruelest, most brutal religion ever recorded, yet not surprisingly, since it is so obviously the work of the devil, it is currently the object of an intense rehabilitation campaign. This campaign is not being conducted by a handful of radical Native-American groups, but proceeds mainly from Academia, from the secular Humanist Establishment, and is of course seconded by the Masonic, anti-Catholic government in Mexico itself. Again Brother Eymard:

> "Don José Lopez Portillo, the President of Mexico, explains to Michel Gabrysiak for Figaro magazine (February 16, 1980), the 'cultural' notion of sacrifice: 'There are two attitudes to sacrifice in all cultures. It is always a response to mystery, to the unknowable. Christ sacrifices himself alone and all others are beneficiaries. With us, it is not the same (!)'. The Indian kills or dies; the two possibilities exist, with total absence of egotistic motive, in order to attempt a solution to the mystery. That is how I feel it and that is why I am very moved by the infinite generosity of pre-Columbian mysticism.' This man rules a people that is 95 per cent Catholic and he dares to say: 'With us, it is not the same'! In whose name is he speaking, I wonder, and with what dark design?"[5]

The only other god in the Aztec pantheon that need concern us here is Quetzalcoatl, the Feathered Serpent. "As a youth, Topiltzin studied for the priesthood and eventually

Our Lady appeared atop the same hill, behind the old Basilica, where the mother-goddess Tonantzin or Coatlicue (left) was worshipped with the sacrifice of women victims

became a high priest of Quetzalcoatl, or the Feathered Serpent, the very ancient god of Teotihuacan and the patron of learning and civilized skills. When Topiltzin ascended the Toltec throne, he changed his own name to Quetzalcoatl. This was not an act of self-deification; high priests of the time were often called by the names of the gods they worshipped. But the change of name causes endless confusion. Both ancient Indian legend-makers and modern historians have often mistaken Topiltzin- Quetzalcoatl, the man, for Quetzalcoatl, the god."[6] Also confusing is the fact that sometimes Quetzalcoatl is considered a type of the true Savior Christ, and at other times of the false savior, Anti-Christ.

In a happy phrase, Eusebius of Caesarea (c. 340) calls the pagan Graeco-Roman civilization a "preparation for the Gospel." It might seem surprising, but the same thing can be said of the Aztec civilization. St. Paul says that the natural world points to the existence of the one true God. "For the invisible things of Him, from the creation of the world, are clearly seen, being understood by the things that are made; His eternal power also, and divinity: so that they are inexcusable" (Rom. 1:20), and that all men have the natural law, the ten commandments, engraved in their hearts (Rom. 2:14, 15). Also the Aztecs had a vague remembrance of the primitive revelation made originally to Adam and Eve. They had once worshipped Ometecuhtli, the one Supreme God, creator of the world, but He had been pushed into the background by the sun and moon and other deities.

"It is not generally known that the true God had already made His existence known through a message sent by His angel to Nezahualcoyotl, King of Texcoco, in 1464. This king abandoned the pagan religion and built temples in which he worshipped the true God, praying before altars containing offerings of flowers and incense. Just before his death Nezahualcoyotl made a great speech ending with these words, 'How deeply I regret that I am not able to understand the will of the great God, but I believe the time will come when he will be known and adored by all the inhabitants of this land.'

"Nezahualcoyotl's son Nezhualpili who succeeded him was the very image of his father. His devotion to the true God was rewarded in being blessed by acknowledgement as the wisest man of his era. Just before he died in 1515, he terrified the emperor Montezuma by telling him he had a dream a few days before in which it was made known to him that Montezuma was soon to lose his throne to invaders from across the sea who were going to bring the true religion. It was occurrences such as these, intensified by prophecies made known to his sister, the Princess Papantzin in 1509, that induced Montezuma to surrender his huge Aztec empire to Cortes in 1521, much to the consternation of secular historians."[7]

But the most amazing story is that of the god Quetzalcoatl, the feathered serpent, worshipped as the evening star, Venus, and once thought to have appeared as a comet that looked like a flying serpent. The historian Warren Carroll writes:

"Quetzalcoatl was one of the old gods; Topiltzin was his high priest and so took his name. But the chief god of the Toltecs was Tezatlipoca, Smoking Mirror, the lord of darkness, who demanded human sacrifice. Topiltzin taught that the true God wanted no such thing; that He was of light, not darkness; that He wanted men to live, to serve Him, and to be chaste, not to be slain in His name.

"Did Ce Acatl Topiltzin know - or did he simply hope? Only God knows.

"Tezcatlipoca and his adherents expelled Topiltzin, first from Tula, the Toltec capital, and then from Cholula. About the year 987

of the Christian era he crossed the sea to Yucatan and spent the rest of his life among the Mayas. But there was a prophecy that he would return from the eastern sea to reclaim what had been his and to resume the leadership of his people and their descendants...

"As it happened, the prophecy was true...if Quetzalcoatl be read as the name given to Christ by a desperate people lost in darkness."[8]

In the 52 year cycle of the Aztec calendar, the year one reed was dedi-

Aztecs adoring one of their many gods. The Quetzalcoatl prophecy about the true God proved true when Cortés and the Spaniards first set foot on Mexican soil, April 22, 1519.

cated to Quetzalcoatl, and his special Feast Day was 9 wind. April 22, 1519 was a 1 reed, 9 wind day, and it was on this day that Cortes first set foot in Mexico. It was Good Friday and he called the place where he landed Vera Cruz. Montezuma, his priests and his court, all devotees of Quetzalcoatl's enemy, Tezcatlipoca, the god of darkness, were paralyzed with fear. It was this Providential "preparation for the Gospel" which made the Conquest of Mexico by just a handful of Spanish Catholics possible.

The Theology of Our Lady of Guadalupe:

The Apparition

There is no need to retell here the beautiful story of Our Lady's Apparition to Juan Diego. It is sufficient to say that it is one of the most charming and tender dialogues between Our Lady and one of her children ever recorded. Just the simple reading of the story was enough to bring one person of good will, the editor and publisher, Coley Taylor, co-author of *The Dark Virgin*, into the Church.

"As he pored over the story of how Our Lady appeared to the poor unlettered Juan Diego, leaving to this day the tangible evidence of her appearance in the miraculous image, he found himself examining the sixteenth-century Aztec's story with the standards of a twentieth- century New York editor and publisher.

"'The fact that Juan Diego forgot completely his appointment with the Blessed Virgin on December 11, and that when he did remember it the next day, on his way to get a priest for his dying uncle, he tried to dodge her - this is charming, and funny, and couldn't have been invented.'

"Equally convincing, he believes, is Juan Diego's confused attempts at small talk when the Virgin intercepted him. 'He asked how she felt, if she had slept well. This couldn't have been inserted by some devout writer. An editor can spot what's phony in a narrative.'

"He also recalled that when Juan Diego discovered the Castilian roses and brought them to the Virgin, she took them out of his tilma and 'rearranged them.'

"'This is very authentic,' observed Mr. Taylor. 'Here she showed her human nature and did what every woman would have done.'"[9]

In her message to Juan Diego Our Lady disclosed three great theological prerogatives, namely that she is the Mother of God, the Mother of the Church, and the Mediatrix of All Graces. "Be it known and understood by you, the smallest of my children, that I am the Ever Virgin Holy Mary, Mother of the true God from whom all life has come of the Creator, close to whom is everything, the Lord of heaven and earth."[10]

The Divine Maternity is the foundation of all Our Lady's glorious prerogatives. Sister Simone Watkin, O.S.B. writes: "Just as the divine maternity is related to the hypostatic union, the spiritual motherhood of Mary proceeds from the dogma of the divine motherhood. In conceiving Jesus, the Head of the Mystical Body, Mary necessarily becomes the spiritual mother of His Members."[11] Our Lady is the Mother of the Church, the Mystical Body of Christ, and since she is the Mother of the Mediator, she is also the Mediatrix of All Graces. "I ardently desire that a temple be built for me here, where I can show and offer all my love, compassion, help and protection, for I am your merciful mother. Here I wish to hear and help you, and all who dwell in this land and all those others who love me, and invoke and place their confidence in me; and to hear your complaints and remedy all your sorrows, hardships and sufferings."[12]

The first apparition of Our Lady to Juan Diego took place on December 9, and the remaining apparitions all occurred within the octave of the Immaculate Conception.

"The Bishop asked for a 'sign' or proof that it is the very Mother of God who had requested a church at Tepeyac. The proof he received he could never have dreamed of nor dared to request. She presented her portrait, painted by the hand of God in lifelike roseate on the thin cloak of her Indian ambassador, Juan Diego. Saintly Bishop Zumárraga dropped to his knees before it, a converted doubting Thomas, gazed at the miracle and in ecstasy cried out, 'Es la Immaculada! It is the Immaculate Virgin!'"[13]

Finally Father Harold Rahm, S.J. in his excellent *Am I Not Here*, brings out yet another theological aspect of the apparition often completely ignored today.

"One other dogmatic point is noteworthy: Our Lady sent Juan Diego to the visible spiritual head and hierarchical ruler *of New Spain. '...and so my intention may be known, go now to the* house of

The saintly first bishop of Mexico, Fray Juan de Zumárraga, who cried out when the Image on theTilma was revealed, "It is the Immaculate Virgin." It was to him, the official representative of the Church, that Our Lady sent Juan Diego to carry out her wishes.

the Bishop *of Mexico...Now hear my words, my dear son, and go and do everything carefully and quickly.' Juan Diego prostrated himself on the ground before her, made answer and said: 'My Holy One, my Lady, I will go now and fulfill your command.'*

"The Holy Spirit animates the body of the Church invisibly with the Divine Life that is the life of grace imparted to the members of the Church through their head, Jesus Christ. Yet, in the Church this invisible life is not independent of the visible and exterior structure of the Church as a society made up of men. It was Christ's will that the Church carry on His work as a visible, organized society, like a city set on a mountain, since the Church was to be the necessary means of salvation for all men."[14]

The Tilma.

Our Lady printed her beautiful image on Juan Diego's tilma or ayate in what for the Indians was more than a picture, but also a beautiful sermon. Father Rahm comments:

"The Indians saw something in the Image of Our Lady that the Spaniards did not comprehend. In that period, the Indians did their

writing in hieroglyphics, so to them the Image was a 'hieroglyphic letter.' The fact that the natives 'read' the picture is most important in understanding the purpose of Our Lady's Apparitions...

"To the Indians, the image depicted a beautiful Lady standing in front of the sun, a sign to them that she was greater than the sun god (Huitzilopochtli), whom they worshipped. The crescent beneath her feet showed that their moon god (Tezcatlipoca) was less than nothing since she was standing on it."[15]

The feathered serpent, Quetzalcoatl, the planet Venus, has become just one of the many stars in Our Lady's mantle.

"The significance of her words, the meaning of her garments, and her whole appearance on Juan Diego's tilma were perfectly clear to the Indians.

"The Indians noted that the lady was not of this world, for a young child with wings was holding her aloft with his two arms. At her throat was a brooch, with a small black cross in the center, reminding them that this was the emblem of the Spanish Friars, and there was One greater than she.

"The 'reading' of the Sacred image brought whole tribes from all over Mexico, led by their chiefs and rulers, to be received into the Faith. And so it happened that the worship of pagan idols was overcome.

"The foregoing facts make it easier to understand the psychology of the natives of Mexico. The Spaniards could not comprehend the reason for making human sacrifices, and consequently, it was most difficult to convince the Indians that they should abandon the practice. But God, who read their hearts and minds, sent the Virgin Mary. Thus it was the Virgin Mother's appearances to Juan Diego, her words: 'I am the ever Virgin Mary, Mother of the true God,' the miraculous appearance of her Image on his tilma and what the Indians read in this 'picture-letter' - that converted more than 8,000,000 natives in seven years to the Catholic Faith."[16]

Genesis 3:15 and Apocalypse 12.

The Spanish were quick to notice that Our Lady was the woman of the Apocalypse clothed with the sun and the moon under her feet. Apocalypse 12 is the same vision as that of Genesis 3:15, since Our Lady is being attacked by a great red dragon who is identified as Satan. But it has only been emphasized recently that Our Lady is also the Woman of Genesis. Our Lady appeared to Juan Bernadino, Juan Diego's uncle, and cured him of his sickness, and told him of her miraculous image and what she wanted it called. "At the same time the lady told him that as soon as he saw the bishop he must reveal to him the miraculous manner in which she had effected his cure and that he should refer to her using her proper name, which would also be the proper name for her blessed image, the ever Virgin Holy Mary of Guadalupe."[17]

Guadalupe is a famous shrine in Estremadura in Spain. Both Bishop Zumárraga and Hernan Cortes were from Estremadura, and there is still displayed an ex voto of a golden scorpion given by Cortes in thanksgiving for his recovery from that insect's sting. But Our Lady of Guadalupe of Estremadura is a statue of a Mother and Child, while Our Lady of Guadalupe of Mexico is a painting of an Immaculata.

The problem has recently been solved by scholars of the Aztec language, who have discovered that the Spanish word Guadalupe (it is actually Arabic meaning "river of the wolf") is similar in sound to Aztec words meaning "she who will crush the serpent." The Aztec scholars differ slightly among themselves on just what Aztec words Our Lady used, but I personally prefer "*Cotallope* (*Coatl* snake and *llope* tread on): 'Who treads on the snake.'"[18] I think it is Providential that the

The Immaculate Conception statue in the Estremadura Shrine in Spain has a striking similarity to the Image of Our Lady of Guadalupe.

name Guadalupe could mean one thing to the Spaniards and another to the Indians. The holy name of Mary has different meanings in different languages, Lady, Star of the Sea, etc. So the name Guadalupe simultaneously reassured the Spaniards and consoled the Indians. But I suspect that Bishop Zumárraga knew the true state of affairs. "Father P. Mariano Cuevas, S.J., in his book recording the events of 1531 to 1541 prints a Zumárragan letter which reveals his rejoicing in 'the redemption of the land through the words of the Immaculate Virgin Mary to Juan Bernadino, "I am the Immaculate Conception, she who has crushed the head of the serpent".'"[19]

The destruction of Satan's kingdom in Mexico in just a few short years was due primarily to Our Lady's beautiful image not made with hands on the tilma of Juan Diego. One is reminded of the prophecy in Daniel concerning another acheiropoeton. "Thus thou sawest, till a stone was cut out of a mountain without hands: and it struck the statue upon the feet thereof that were of iron and of clay, the brass, the silver and the gold broken to pieces together, and became like the chaff of a summer's thrashing-floor, and there was no place found for them: but the stone that struck the statue, became a great mountain, and filled the whole earth" (Daniel 2:34, 35).

Let me conclude this section with just one more point. In 1325 a few thousand Aztecs established themselves on an island in Lake Texcoco. "here they had sighted their sign of destiny" 'Perched on a cactus was an eagle devouring a snake.' Today the eagle devouring a snake is the coat of arms of the nation and can be seen on Mexican currency and the National Flag."[20] In Apocalypse 12 the woman clothed with the sun is given the wings of an eagle to escape the fury of the serpent. On the miraculous tilma, Our Lady of Guadalupe, "who treads on the snake," stands on an angel with eagle's wings. Should this interpretation be valid, the symbol is indeed a fitting one for a nation that was once the land of Satan, but now belongs to Mary.

A statuary group of native Americans paying homage to their Queen, Mary of Guadalupe. Inset, woodcut from the first book published on Guadalupe, showing the Woman of the Apocalypse standing over the cactus, taking the place of the snake, with the eagle wings holding her up — all symbols of Mexico.

The Anti-Apparitionists

Given the fact that Our Lady of Guadalupe is a vision of Genesis 3:15, it should not seem strange that it has been the object of constant attack, indeed it would be strange if this were not so. St. Simeon prophesied "and thy own soul a sword shall pierce, that out of many hearts, thoughts may be revealed" (Luke 2:35). The Mexicans, charmingly it seems to me, divide the world into Guadalupanos and anti-apparitionistas. Fr. José Romero, S.J. says of the anti-apparitionists, "Their names have passed into history like a black stain which no one and nothing will be able to erase."[21]

It would serve little purpose here to go through them all, especially the older ones. I would like to concentrate on two of the recent ones, Jacques Lafaye of the Sorbonne and D. Scott Rogo, a leading authority on what is called "paranormal" phenomena. But since Lafaye makes so much of it, I had better mention one of the more bizarre cases which occurred in 1795, that of the Dominican Fray Servando de Mier, and the "scholar" José Borunda. Mier's astounding thesis was that the miraculous tilma did not belong to Juan Diego but to the Apostle St. Thomas whose visit to Mexico in Apostolic times had been transformed into the legend of Quetzalcoatl:

"Borunda, the antiquarian, had indeed seen visions in examining the famous 'Aztec Calendar Stone' recently unearthed from the plaza fronting the cathedral in Mexico City. The stone, like a crystal ball, told Borunda that St. Thomas had come to Mexico some five years after the death of Christ. It also revealed that the Spaniards would come much later.

"In the resulting delirium, Borunda saw St. Thomas building a temple in the high sierra of Tenyuca to enshrine his miraculous cloak with the impress of the Virgin. He also saw Indians coming to vener-

ate it, and later becoming apostates and trying vainly to efface the image. St. Thomas then hid it. It would appear again to Juan Diego, ten years after the coming of the Spaniards. The Indian would take it, along with the miraculous roses, to the Bishop, and ask that a church be built in the sierra to house the miraculous cloak of St. Thomas.

"The censors handed in their report. The Archbishop then declared Mier's history of Our Lady of Guadalupe false, apocryphal and improbable."[21]

Let me just add one amusing story concerning another of the early anti- apparitionists, José Ignacio Bartolache, who to disprove the miraculous nature of the tilma of Juan Diego, had an exact copy made on the same burlap-like material, maguey fibre, and with much fanfare, had it hung in the chapel built on the site of Our Lady's final apparition to Juan Diego:

"The copy by Gutiérrez was placed in the Chapel of the Well, as contracted under glass. The ceremony took place on Our Lady's feast of September 12, 1789. After seven short years, the painting was so unsightly and discolored that, on June 8, 1796, it was quietly removed to the sacristy. An eyewitness of the time. Francisco Solano, described the pitiful condition of the painting. The gold had dimmed and partly peeled off; the blue-green of the Virgin's mantle had turned either a blackish-green or an ashen color like rust; and the salmon-pink of the tunic had turned white. Where the paint had peeled off, the weave was exposed and some threads had broken. In this sorry state, the painting was given to the convent of the Third Order of Carmelites in Mexico City, where it passed into oblivion."[22]

Jacques Lafaye's book Quetzalcoatl and Guadalupe: The Formation of the Mexican National Consciousness 1531-1813, was presented as a thesis for a doctoral degree at the University of Paris in 1974, and was promptly translated into English by the University of Chicago Press in 1976. Lafaye's incredible thesis is that the original image of Our Lady of Guadalupe was the statue of a Mother and Child venerated under the same title at Estremadura in Spain. But around 1648 Fr. Miguel Sanchez, the author of the first book in Spanish on Our Lady of Guadalupe, substituted a painting, which was probably an ex voto left in the church by an unknown Indian, and invented the whole story of the apparition. He also fabricated the earlier Indian narratives such as the *Nichan Mopohua*. His motive, according to Lafaye, was to protest Spanish colonialism, and to substitute an indigenous Mexican Virgin for a foreign Spanish one. This was the beginning of what Lafaye calls the formation of the Mexican national consciousness.

I won't bother going into the details of Lafaye's historical arguments which are mostly a rehash of earlier anti-apparitionists like Bartolache and Teresa de Mier. Let me just give one Lafaye original. He is trying to establish that the image was originally a statue. In 1582, Miles Philips, a captured English pirate, visited the chapel and described a large statue, but didn't mention a painting. Brother Leies writes:

"The Spaniards' devotion to Our Lady of Guadalupe certainly impressed Miles Philips. What caught his pirate's eye was the life-size silver image of Our Lady and the many silver lamps that seemed to multiply before his eager gaze (there should have been but seventy!)...and he completely omits any mention of the sacred image, since his eyes readily fixed on the large silver image, the gift of the wealthy Alonso de Villaseca, as mentioned in the diary of Juan Bautista."[23]

The large silver statue, which of course caught the greedy pirate's eye, was an ex voto which was later melted down to make silver candle sticks for the altar. Lafaye's book abounds in this kind of preposterous argument. Lafaye casually dismisses the miraculous preservation of Juan Diego's tilma for over 450 years:

"The miraculous preservation of sacred images, far from being a special attribute of the divine ayate of Tepeyac, seems to be a cliché, of pious traditions. In his Journey to Covadonga, Ambrosio de Morales, a priest sent to the sanctuary by King Philip to inquire into the tradition, wrote: "It is said that this church was founded by King Alfonso the Chaste, and that it has remained miraculously in the same state ever since, without any decay of its wood." Morales was skeptical and saw "clear signs of new construction"; but he accompanied his doubt with the reflection,..."God can perform the greatest miracles."...When he reports the discovery of an image of the Ecce Homo at Zebu by a soldier who was digging the foundations for his

house, Fray Gaspar de San Agustin describes the event as a "miraculous discovery," and accompanies his account with this reflection: 'A very holy image of an Ecce Homo has been found, a wooden sculpture very well preserved for having lain so many years in such a place.'"[24]

But the main thrust of Lafaye's attack on the cult of Our Lady of Guadalupe is that it, and the cult of St. Thomas, are examples of syncretism between the Aztec religion and Christianity. Regarding the cult of Our Lady he writes:

"One of the fundamental couples of the Mexican pantheon, or rather one of the dominant expressions (especially in the minds of the ruling elite) of the universal creative principle, is Tonantzin-Quetzalcoatl, whose creole avatars are equally inseparable. From pre-Columbian times they appear linked together as the two faces, male and female, of the primary creative principle...

"The importance of the sanctuaries is primordial; on the topographic base of sanctuaries, the process of syncretism between the great divinities of ancient Mexico and the saints of Christianity worked itself out. The most notable example is precisely that of the hill of Tepeyac, first a place of pilgrimage and sanctuary of Tonantzin-Cihuacoatl and later of Our Lady of Guadalupe."[25]

And regarding the cult of St. Thomas:

"Among the various Indian divinities identified with Saint Thomas, the most representative of Indian spirituality in its most evolved forms was the Mexican god-hero Ce Acatl Quetzalcoatl-Topiltzin, called also Ehecatl, and identified with the Morning Star, Tlauicalpantecuhtli. Quetzalcoatl-St. Thomas is thus the most outstanding example of syncretism between the cosmological myths of ancient America and Christianity, the extreme point of contact reached by the two worlds in their advance toward each other. Saint Thomas of America was also one of the roots of the American consciousness, a consciousness that even now remains charged with charismatic certainty and messianic hope."[26]

But nobody ever took the pathetic Quetzalcoatl-St. Thomas theory of Borunda and Mier seriously, and for Lafaye to give it such prominence is ridiculous. Lafaye goes on to claim that this syncretism of the Aztec religion and Christianity is no longer relevant in today's society. Joseph Campbell, an ex-Catholic and an authority on comparative mythology writes:

"All religions have been true for their time. If you can recognize the enduring aspect of their truth and separate it from the temporal applications, you've got it...But today there are no boundaries. The only mythology that is valid today is the mythology of the planet - and we don't have such a mythology. The closest thing I know to a planetary mythology is Buddhism, which sees all beings as Buddha beings. The only problem is to come to the recognition of that."[27]

This syncretism and relativism of Lafaye and Campbell regarding religion and truth are of course, directed primarily against the absolute truth of the Catholic faith and its necessity for salvation.

D. Scot Rogo is today's leading so-called psychic scientist or parapsychologist, and is the author of more than ten books on the subject. His most recent book, *Miracles: A Parascientific Inquiry Into Wondrous Phenomena* discusses both Our Lady of Guadalupe and the Holy Shroud of Turin. Unlike Lafaye Rogo accepts the historicity of the apparitions to Juan Diego, but rejects the supernatural origin of the Image, and indeed believes that all miracles do not come from God, but "occur through the agency of the human mind and its psychic capabilities."[28] Rogo's technique is to begin with a well-known Catholic miracle, and follow it with several non-Christian, and even what he calls "secular analogues."

"The talent to perform a miracle may be a natural human potential not just the province of saints and mystics. A complimentary theme is that while the great saints of the Catholic Church were probably genuinely psychic, no single world religion has a franchise on the miraculous. Catholicism's saints; the fakirs and holy men of the East; the shamans of Alaska, Africa, and Mongolia; the witch doctors of the American Indians - all possess similar abilities."[29]

The conclusion Rogo draws from this is, "It would be clear from these comparisons is that it would be fruitless to argue that the miracles of Jesus and the saints demonstrate the supremacy of Christianity, since adherents of other world religions could make equally valid claims for the divinity of their own sacred individuals."[30] This statement is remarkably similar to the Pharisees claim that Jesus cast out devils by Beelzebub the prince of devils, which Our Lord called the sin against the Holy Ghost, meaning that they were making it impossible for the Holy Ghost to bear witness to the truths of Our Lord's teachings.

As I read Rogo's account of the miraculous Image of Guadalupe, followed by his three or four pale and ephemeral non-Christian and secular analogues, I was reminded of Moses before Pharaoh. When Aaron threw down his rod it turned into a serpent, Pharaoh's magicians "by Egyptian enchantments and certain secrets" did the same, and their rods also turned into serpents. "But Aaron's rod devoured their rods" (Exodus 7:10-12). The magicians were able to match Moses for the first two plagues, but dropped out on the third, which means, I think, that the seed of Satan can perform "miracles" up to a point, but God always arranges it in such a way, that only a person of bad will like Pharaoh, will be deceived by them. Anti-Christ will perform great signs and wonders (Matthew 24:24), but the elect will not be deceived if they remain close to Mary. Concerning the apparition itself Rogo writes:

"Yet there can be no doubt that Marian visitations follow a rather concise pattern. They seem to be cosmic reactions to threats against the religious and social status quo of the time. Her appearances in Mexico apparently quelled a potential Indian uprising...

"It was the great Swiss psychologist Carl Jung (1875-1961) who first developed the concept of the archetype. While studying the rich folklore of a number of different cultures, Jung was struck by the fact that many societies throughout the world have developed similar symbols and legends. For instance, most cultures associate 'darkness' with evil and 'light' with good. Likewise, the bird is often used as the symbol of the soul.

"Jung eventually discovered that human beings, no matter in what country they live or during what period of time, seem to share a common, unconscious, symbolic 'language.' He called these shared symbols archetypes, and considered them to have been genetically inherited from the beginnings of mankind. Related to the concept of the archetype is what Jung called the collective unconscious, which is one of the most misunderstood of his theories. The 'collective unconscious' does not actually refer to a supermind to which we are connected on some cosmic level, nor is it a 'universal unconscious.' By 'collective

unconscious' Jung meant a primitive level of mind in which we all think in the same way by the use of similar symbols or archetypes.

"It is conceivable that linked to these universal archetypes are culturally determined religious 'images' that become limited archetypes in societies that share a common religious background. In Western culture, for instance, we invariably imagine God to be a bearded old man seated on a throne, Jesus as a bearded man about the age of thirty, and Mary as a radiant queen. We can therefore construct a theory about the nature of Marian apparitions by uniting the concept of culturally determined archetypes with the theory (held by many parapsychologists) that all of us are telepathically linked to one another at some subliminal level of mind.

"The key to understanding Marian apparitions may be in their tendency to occur at times of social and/or political crisis. At such times of stress, some form of mass telepathic communication may occur in the collective unconscious of the threatened culture. This may lead to the formation of a 'group mind,' which, in turn, results in the projection of a Marian visitation - a process similar to the one which may have produced the Guadalupe miracle of 1531."[31]

As I continued reading Rogo's claims for the "science of

A Mexican couple view the mural of Our Lady appearing to Juan Diego on Dec. 12, 1532, located in the chapel on the top of the hill where he heard the soft and melodious songs of many birds.

parapsychology," I was reminded of François Mauriac's reaction on hearing a lecture on the "science" of evolutionism: "What this professor says is far more incredible than what we poor Christians believe."[32]

Rogo compares the Guadalupe apparition to, among others, that of Our Lady of Pontmain in France in 1870:

"The Pontmain affair supports the 'archetype theory' of Marian apparitions which was formulated earlier in this chapter. At some deep level of mind, the residents of Pontmain must have been aware of the threat posed to their town by the advancing Prussian troops. This danger could have caused a vivid unconscious preoccupation with the Virgin Mother in her archetypal image as protectress and intermediary between Man and God. This may ultimately have produced a mass psychic effect...that resulted in the projection of the image of the BVM into the night sky. (Note the figure was more of a projection or holograph-like image than any living presence.) The unconscious minds of the villagers may then have telepathically picked up the information that the Prussian high command had decided to spare Pontmain, and the figure adjusted her appearance and message accordingly."[33]

Lafaye for his part compares Our Lady of Guadalupe in Mexico to Our Lady of Guadalupe in Estremadura:

"We can only say that in the case of two peoples, inhabiting the same spiritual world, comparable historical ordeals, threatening the existence of the community, inspired the rise of analogous mythical responses at an interval of more than two centuries. The historian also notes the fact of emigration from the old places of pilgrimage; to the extent that they promise salvation to the community, the gods are found accompanying men in their migrations. To New Spain, with the delay of more than a century that is normal in the transfer of a holy place, came 'New Guadalupe,' like a reserve of spiritual oxygen needed by the new society to affirm its identity and stimulate its development."[34]

Lafaye and Rogo claim that their attacks on Our Lady of Guadalupe are scientific, since they are based on Jungian psychology, which they say is scientific. But I think that Jung's system is not scientific but religious, in fact it is, to use their own jargon, the latest avatar of Gnosticism. If the evolutionists can reject the scientific findings of the creationists on the grounds that they are not scientific but religious, we should be able to do the same with the Jungians. The acclaimed biographer of Jung, Laurens van der Post writes:

"Jung was back with that concern he always felt from the moment of the first great dream experienced at the age of three. But never before had he realized so clearly how the future of mankind depended on a rediscovery of his capacity for religious experience accessible in a twentieth-century idiom and not in the archaic, dogmatic, doctrinal conceptualized way in which it had been imposed on him for centuries, It is remarkable how always those who in the end could gain most from his work misunderstood and attacked what he was trying to do, like the churches and institutions of science. He knew, he protested over and over again, that only religion could replace religion."[35]

In 1947 a Gnostic library dating from the 3rd or 4th century A.D. was discovered at Nag Hammadi in Egypt. Jung was presented with parts of Codex I, the only codice to leave the country. John Dart comments:

"Though the persistence of the Jung Institute and the presentation to Jung might have seemed surprising to outsiders, the actions would not have been to the admirers of the psychoanalyst. Jung made a serious study of the Gnostics from 1916 to 1926, attracted by what he saw as the Gnostic writers' confrontations with 'the primal world of the unconscious.' He ended that effort with an unsatisfied feeling, largely because of the paucity of accounts, stemming mostly from the Gnostic opponents, the church fathers. And Jung believed the Gnostics too remote in time, without any psychohistorical link to the present. Only later, by his own account, through his study of the mystical alchemists of the Middle Ages did he find what he considered a bridge between Gnosticism and 'the modern psychology of the unconscious.' Jung credited Sigmund Freud with introducing the classical Gnostic motif of the wicked paternal authority into modern psychology. The evil Creator God of the Gnostics 'reappeared in the Freudian myth of the primal father and the gloomy superego deriving from the father,' Jung said. 'In Freud's myth he became a demon who created a world of disappointments, illusions and suffering.'

"Missing from Freud's system, Jung said, was another essential aspect of Gnosticism - the primordial feminine spirit from another, higher god who gave humans the possibility of spiritual transformation. Writing shortly after Pope Pius XII issued a 1950 papal bull on

the Assumption of the Blessed Virgin Mary, Jung applauded the church for its partial recognition of the feminine aspect of divinity. He said in effect that the bull affirmed that Mary as the Bride is united with the Son in the heavenly bridal chamber, and as Sophia (Wisdom) she is united with the Godhead.

"Through their myth making many Gnostics showed themselves to be 'not so much heretics as theologians,' or even 'psychologists,' asserted Jung. For example, Jung said, the position of respect given by some Gnostic groups to the snake was not as strange as one might think. The snake represents the 'extra-human quality in man,' he said. The cold-blooded, staring serpent expresses man's fear of the inhuman 'and his awe of the sublime, of what is beyond human ken.'"[36]

Three of the Nag Hammadi codices, *The Apocryphon of John, The Nature of the Archons,* and *On the Origin of the World,* contain Gnostic versions of the Garden of Eden story in which the serpent is the hero and God the villain. This is exactly the position of Jungian psychology, concerning the story of Adam and Eve. I could give many illustrations to prove this point, but let me give just one from a Jungian psychiatrist, Edward Edinger:

"The myth depicts the birth of consciousness as a crime which alienates man from God and from his original preconscious wholeness. The fruit is clearly symbolic of consciousness. It is the fruit of the tree of the knowledge of good and evil, which means that it brings awareness of the opposites, the specific feature of consciousness. Thus, according to this myth and the theological doctrines that rest on it, consciousness is the original sin, the original hybris, *and the root cause of all evil in human nature. However others have understood it differently. The Ophites, a Gnostic sect, worshipped the serpent. They had essentially the same view as modern psychology. To them the serpent represented the spiritual principle symbolizing redemption from bondage to the demiurge that created the Garden of Eden and would keep man in ignorance. The serpent is the principle of gnosis, knowledge or emerging consciousness. The serpent's temptation represents the urge to self-realization in man and symbolizes the principle of individuation. Some Gnostic sects even identified the serpent in the Garden of Eden with Christ..."*

"I believe with the Ophites that it is one sided to depict Adam and Eve as shameful orchard thieves. Their action could equally be de-

scribed as an heroic one. *They sacrifice the passive comfort of obedi-*
ence for greater consciousness. The serpent does indeed prove to be a
benefactor in the long run if we grant consciousness a greater value
than comfort."[37]

The Gnostic heresy was fortunately almost totally destroyed by St. Irenaeus. In the Introduction to the English
version of his *Against Heresies* the editors write:

"If Julian [the Apostate] had found Gnosticism just made to his hand, and powerful enough to suit his purposes, the whole history of his attempt to revive Paganism would have been widely different. Irenaeus demonstrated its essential unity with the old mythology, and with the heathen systems of philosophy. If the fog and malaria that rose with the Day-star, and obscured it, were speedily dispersed, our author is largely to be identified with the radiance which flowed from the Sun of righteousness, and with the breath of the Spirit that banished them forever."[38]

Jung and his disciples are offering us a broad syncretistic and relativistic base that can absorb all faiths, including the Catholic, provided none of them claims to be the one true faith. The Catholic Modernists and Liberals, it seems to me, have already accepted this status within the confines of secular humanism. Jung's religion seems to made to order for that successor of Julian the Apostate, Anti-Christ.

But the way to rebut false science, or religion masquerading as science, is by true science. Let me turn now to the science of ethnology. Here we learn that the most primitive stage of culture is the Hunter-Gatherer stage in which the outstanding characteristic is its absolute monotheism. There are still scattered remnants of this earliest culture left in remote parts of the world. The next step in the development of culture (I will only mention the two that concern us here) are the patriarchal Higher Hunter and the matriarchal Village-Agricultural stages. In these stages the Supreme Being has been pushed into the background and nature myths have come to the fore. In the Higher Hunter culture the sun is worshipped and animals associated with the sun, like the eagle, are considered totems, that is ancestors of the tribe. In the Village-Agricultural stage the moon and the earth are worshipped, and often the serpent in fertility rites, and strangely it seems to me, it is in this matriarchal culture that human sacrifice occurs for the first time. The Aztec civilization is a blend and development of the Higher Hunter and Village - Agricultural stages.

One of the world's foremost authorities on ethnology, Fr. Wilhelm Schmidt, S.V.D., writes:

"Glancing back over the picture of man's oldest religion as drawn by the historical correlation of ethnology and prehistory, we are immediately impressed by the contrast between our findings and the aprioristic theorizings of the old progressive evolutionists.

"It was affirmed that the development of religion must have started from inferior beginnings; but, since moral monotheism is an intrinsically high form, they argued a priori that this could be only the final result of a long and complicated development, which ultimately produced monotheism. As a matter of fact, however, it is precisely in the oldest stage of culture that we meet monotheism pure and simple; whereas it is exactly in the later stages that monotheism recedes before the onrush of naturism, animism, and magism."[39]

We saw Jacques Lafaye maintain that Quetzalcoatl-Tonantzin, the male and female principles, were the "primordial dualism." But such is not the case. The primitive Hunter-Gatherers have only one Supreme God and a female consort is a later development of the matriarchal Village-Agriculture stage. Father Schmidt:

"...There is a sufficient number of tribes among whom the really monotheistic character of their Supreme Being is clear even to a cursory examination. This is true of the Supreme Being of most Pygmy tribes, so far as we know them; also of the Tierra del Fuegians, the primitive Bushmen, the Kurnai, Kulin and Yuin of South-East Australia, the peoples of the Arctic culture, except the Koryaks, and well-nigh all the primitives of North America...

"In nearly every separate area of the primitive culture the First Father plays an important part, especially in the initiation ceremonies; originally he and the First Mother were the parents of the race. Owing to the later influence of the matrilinear cultures, he develops a lunar character, is brought into connexion with the moon and not uncommonly obscures the Supreme Being or blends with him. Where contact has been established with the solar mythology of the totemistic patrilineal culture, the young and powerful morning sun is represented as the child of the Supreme Being, who later becomes identified with the ageing evening sun and is obscured by the morning sun...

"Yet another source of a multiplicity of superior beings is the family relationships of the Supreme Being, when he appears with a wife and children. But we must make the following observations. In the first place, there is a number of the peoples of the primitive culture who give their Supreme Being neither wife nor children, and even

think it shocking or absurd to inquire if he has them. Such peoples are to be found in each of the several primitive circles and generally are the most ancient races of these circles; this is sufficient to make it probable in a high degree that this is the more nearly original state of things. Among these peoples are the Negrillos of Africa, the Negritos of the Philippines, the Kurnai of South-East Australia, the Samoyeds, the primitive Eskimo, the Ainu - the last three belong to the Arctic culture - and practically all the North American primitives. But in the case of the Supreme Being having acquired a wife and children, we can prove that these are later accretions from solar or lunar myths, and to some extent also from older sources than these."[40]

The facts discovered by the science of ethnology uphold the teaching of the Church concerning a primitive revelation made to Adam and Eve, which was kept almost intact by some of their descendants, but corrupted in others. So Jung's theory concerning the origin of religion by "archetypes" arising in the "collective unconscious" is wrong, since it does not square with the teaching of the Church concerning a primitive revelation, nor with the findings of ethnology. The reason for the similarity in myths all over the world is due not to the genetic nature of the archetypes, but to diffusion. As the Hunter-Gatherers spread over the world they retained their own culture, as did the Higher Hunter and Village-Agriculturalists. In scattered pockets of the world these primitive cultures are discovered even today. Even the Jungian, Joseph Campbell, admits the diffusion theory as a possible alternative to Jung's theory of genetic archetypes:

MOYERS: How do you explain these similarities?

CAMPBELL: There are two explanations, One explanation is that the human psyche is essentially the same all over the world. The psyche is the inward experience of the human body, which is essentially the same in all human beings, with the same organs, the same instincts , the same impulses, the same conflicts, the same fears. Out of this common ground have come what Jung called the archetypes, which are the common ideas of myths...

"Now there is a counter-theory of diffusion to account for the similarity of myths. For instance, the art of tilling the soil goes forth from the area in which it was first developed, and along with it goes a mythology that has to do with fertilizing the earth, with planting

44

and bringing up the food plants - some such myths as just described, of killing a deity, cutting it up, burying its members, and having the food plants grow. Such a myth will accompany an agricultural or planting tradition. But you won't find it in a hunting culture. So there are historical as well as psychological aspects of this problem of the similarity of myths."[41]

Let me conclude this section with one final quote from Jacques Lafaye:

"...The tenacious hold of the cult of Guadalupe in a Mexico that is profoundly de-Christianized (at least in its urban milieu) deserves the attention of students of religious sociology. No less interesting is the question of the profound meaning, from the point of view of the national consciousness, of the Quetzalcoatl myth as a literary theme. The poets in particular have been fascinated by this mythical image of the Indian past: besides Mexicans like Garcia Pimental, Agusti Bartra, Carlos Fuentes, we find the Chilean poetess Gabriela Mistral and D.H. Lawrence. Without seeking to anticipate the conclusions of a study that may cast a surer light on the 'Mexican soul,' that is, on Mexican society, I may observe that the literary renaissance of Quetzalcoatl is contemporaneous with the rise of the indigenist movement in the 1920s and 30s.

"If we accept the judgment of a psychologist of penetrating vision, according to whom, 'The history of cultures is summed up in the process of the creation of mythical images, their dogmatization, and their destruction,' we must admit that the viceregal culture inherited from New Spain is breathing its last in modern Mexico. Some day Guadalupe will become an extinct star, like the moon, with which she is associated; it would be fascinating to study the emergence of the mythical image that will replace her. Quetzalcoatl, by contrast, more closely linked to Mexican polytheism, and now detached from his temporary twin, St. Thomas, seems to have a better chance of a future 're-charge' in a laicized society like that of present-day Mexico. If the myth of Quetzalcoatl has retained its vitality through-out its successive avatars, in colonial and independent Mexico alike, it is because he is the symbolic expression of the Indian past which the creole consciousness sought to revive from its ashes so as to build upon it the claim of Mexican independence. Evoking the origins of the Mexican revolution, José Vasconcelos wrote that 'Quetzalcoatl-Madero won a victory without precedent.' After Madero, the Mexican people believed that it saw in Quetzalcoatl-Cardenas the new incarnation of the Indian messiah come from the depths of the ages, a Phoenix who

is reborn with each new 'sun' from the ashes of the preceding sun. Like the aspiration for justice, Quetzalcoatl is imperishable; no sooner has he been driven away or, like Madero, assassinated by a modern Tezcatlipoca, then he is ready to be reincarnated in the form of a new political chief. Mexico is simultaneously a sacred space, the land of the 'children of Guadalupe,' and, in time, a nostalgic yearning for the lost paradise of Quetzalcoatl, a floating myth ever ready to alight on the Elect."[42]

We could have concluded Lafaye's list of avatars of Quetzalcoatls, with Quetzalcoatl-Anti-Christ. Lafaye's book instead of Quetzalcoatl and Guadalupe, should have been called *The Serpent and the Woman.* Far from being an extinct star, Our Lady of Guadalupe still has her foot on the serpent Quetzalcoatl's head in Mexico. The proof is in the pilgrims that still come by their millions to her Shrine. Here is Blessed Miguel Pro, recently beatified by Pope John Paul II, who was martyred by Quetzalcoatl-Calles:

"During the savage persecution of the Church by the Calles Government in the 1920s, the Basilica was the only Catholic Church in Mexico to remain open. On the Feast of Christ the King, October 31, 1927, at the height of that persecution, when people were shot for demonstrating against the anti-religious regime, more than 200,000 people visited this Shrine.

"Father Miguel Pro, the Jesuit priest and martyr who later died before one of Calles' firing squads, wrote of that unprecedented and dangerous event:

'The pilgrimages began at four o'clock in the morning, and nearly everybody in the city filed past the blessed Image of Our Lady. I could not tear myself away from such a sight!

'Thousands of people went down Peravillo Avenue, either on their knees or barefoot, praying and singing - both rich and poor - the working classes and the upper class...In no time our own choir was engulfed with thousands of people, all acclaiming the Virgin Mary, Christ the King, the Pope, the Bishops!'"[43]

Science and the Miraculous Image

Let us turn now to true science rather than false science, or religion masquerading as science. Like the Holy Shroud of Turin, the miraculous tilma of Juan Diego has been subjected to rigorous scientific scrutiny, especially of late. But we should be very discriminating concerning scientific scrutiny lest there be a repeat of the recent Carbon-14 incident, which threw so many devotees of the Holy Shroud into a panic. We don't need science to tell us that the Holy Shroud or the miraculous tilma are authentic; we have the testimony of the Magisterium and the constant miracles. In 1754 Pope Benedict XIV wrote:

"In it everything is miraculous: an Image emanating from flowers gathered on completely barren soil on which only prickly shrubs can grow; an Image entrusted to a fabric so thin that through it the nave and the people can be seen as easily as through a trellis; an Image in no matter deteriorated, neither in her supreme loveliness, nor in its sparkling colors, by the niter or the neighboring lake, which however, corrodes silver, gold and brass...God has not done likewise to any other nation."[44]

And again in 1945 Pope Pius XII said:

"On the shores of Lake Texcoco flowered the Miracle, and on the cloak of humble Juan Diego was painted a most lovely Portrait, by brushes not of this earth,...a painting which the corrosive work of the centuries was marvelously to respect...[45]

"Hail, O Virgin of Guadalupe! We to whom the admirable disposition of Divine Providence has confided, without taking into consideration Our unworthiness, the sacred treasure of Divine Wisdom on earth, for the salvation of all souls, We again place on your brow the crown which forever puts under your powerful patronage the purity and integrity of the holy faith in Mexico and in all the American continent. For We are certain that, while you are recognized as

Queen and as Mother, America and Mexico will be saved."[46]

The miraculous preservation of the tilma of Juan Diego has also been attested to by continuous miracles. Let me mention just two:

"The Image also could have been seriously damaged one day through the clumsiness of a goldsmith who was cleaning the frame. Nitric acid was spilled and ran down the whole right side of the tilma. Miraculously, the acid lost its bite as it touched the tilma and left but a stained streak, This streak can easily be seen on any good reproduction of the Image.

"And on November 14, 1922, during the height of the Calles persecution, a powerful bomb was placed on the altar of the blessed Image. The huge bronze crucifix was twisted as if made of wax - this crucifix is venerated today in the Basilica. The marble decorations and several windows of the Church were shattered and the bolts holding the heavy gold frame of the Image were loosened yet the glass and the blessed Image were miraculously spared."[47]

But I think that the Church in allowing the miraculous tilma, the Holy Shroud, and of course the Medical Bureau at Lourdes, to be open to the scrutiny of even non-Catholic scientists, is making available a wonderful sign for our unbelieving generation. Any way to come into the Church is a good way. The shepherds came just by seeing Baby Jesus in His Mother's arms (one is reminded of Coley Taylor), while the Magi, the scientists of their day, came by the study of astronomy.

Andrew Lang in his *The Making of Religion* begins his study of miracles with a criticism of the English skeptic, David Hume:

"Hume derided the observation and study of what he called 'Miracles,' in the field of experience, and he looked for an a priori argument which would forever settle the question without examination of the facts. In an age of experimental philosophy, which derided a priori methods, this was Hume's great contribution to knowledge. His famous argument, the joy of many an honest breast, is a tissue of fallacies which might be given for exposure to beginners in logic, as an elementary exercise. In announcing his discovery, Hume amusingly displays the self-complacency and want of humor with which we Scots are commonly charged by our critics.

The twisted crucifix which was standing before the Sacred Image, when a bomb blew off in the old Basilica (right) in a vain attempt by the anti-Catholic elements in Mexico in the twenties to destroy the tilma

"'I flatter myself that I have discovered an argument which, if just, will, with the wise and learned, be an everlasting check to all kinds of superstitious delusions, and consequently will be useful as long as the world endures.'

"He does not expect, however, to convince the multitude. Till the end of the world, 'accounts of miracles and prodigies, I suppose, will be found in all histories, sacred and profane.' Without saying here what he means by a miracle, Hume argues that 'experience is our only guide in reasoning.' He then defines a miracle as 'a violation of the laws of nature.' By 'a law of nature' he means a uniformity, not of all experience, but of such experience as he will deign to admit; while he excludes, without examination, all evidence for experience of the absence of such uniformity. That kind of experience cannot be considered. 'There must be a uniform experience against every miraculous event, otherwise the event would not merit that appellation.' If there be any experience in favor of the event, that experience does not count. A miracle is counter to universal experience, therefore no event is a miracle. If you produce evidence to what Hume calls a miracle (we shall see examples) he replies that the evidence is not valid, unless its falsehood would be more miraculous than the fact. Now no error of human evidence can be more miraculous than a 'miracle.' Therefore there can be no valid evidence for 'miracles.'"[48]

49

Hume is of course seconded in this dogmatic assertion by the whole secular humanist Establishment. Against such arguments the Guadalupanos are fond of quoting Gilbert K. Chesterton in his *Orthodoxy*:

"My belief that miracles have happened in human history is not a mystical belief at all; I believe in them upon human evidences as I do in the discovery of America...Somehow or other an extraordinary idea has arisen that disbelievers in miracles consider them coldly or fairly, while believers in miracles accept them (rightly or wrongly) only because they have some evidence for them. The disbelievers in miracles deny them (rightly or wrongly) because they have a doctrine against them."[49]

In 1616 in preparation for a formal petition to the Holy See for a special Mass and Office for the Feast of Our Lady of Guadalupe, the Cathedral Chapter supervised a careful examination of the holy Image by the most renowned artists and physicians (the scientists of the day) in New Spain. The sworn statement of the artists reads:

"...After having felt with their hands the said painting of the said Most Sacred Image, they were not able to find or discover in it anything except the mysterious or miraculous, and that no one but God Our Lord could create a thing so beautiful and with so many perfections as those they found in the Holy Painting. And they hold without any doubt that it is impossible to size and paint on such a tilma or cactus-linen, and they swear without any reservation: That the figure imprinted on the ayate *or* tilma *of Juan Diego, the said Portrait of Our Lady of Guadalupe, was, and must be attributed to have been a supernatural creation and a secret reserved to the Divine Majesty, and likewise the preservation of the colors and drapery of the robes which make it stand out from the white clouds which are the border and background."[50]*

"So that, having brought to this matter the erudition and fundamentals of reason and science, they derived as legitimate consequence that the perseverance, through so many years, of the liveliness of the colors and the form of the Holy Painting, and the integrity and permanency of the material of the cactus fibre (ayate) - when scientific principles are all against such preservation - could not be due to any natural cause, and that its origin could only be through Him alone Who can perform miraculous effects through the use of all the forces of nature.

"They also made the statement that since there are no green colors at all on the right side of the Holy painting - none in the face, or the hands, or the drapery, or in any other part of the fabric - on the reverse side are to be seen and distinguished very lovely green colors, like those of the leaves of lilies and other plants. Concerning this, these worthy doctors say: 'The understanding wavers, discourse confuses, and the prodigy refers itself to the realm of mystery as Aristotle, Prince of Philosophers, asserts as an incontrovertible principle: Idem, in quantum idem, semper est natum facere idem: That the same element, in the same matter, with the same arrangement, can only produce the same effect.' Why does the color green, which this same tilma bears on its wrong side, not come through at all to the right side? God alone, Who made it, knows why.

"The second observation that they made was that, under examination, the fabric which holds the Holy Image is seen to be hard, rough, and firm on the wrong side, while on the right side it is smooth, glossy and soft, like a silk. Although it is all the same piece of material, the right and wrong sides reveal distinctly different, even completely opposed characteristics.

"Why is it that the roughness and hardness of the coarse-canvas texture of the wrong side do not penetrate to the right side - against all that natural reason and experience teach us and demonstrate about any linen or canvas, which, if wet or dry, cold or hot, coarse or smooth on one side is the same on both sides?

"I am not going to attempt to explain this: I merely refer it to the all-powerful Artisan Who, in creating this Portrait, suspended the ordinary laws and rules of nature, as He did in the instance of the conception of His Blessed Mother, so that it might be known that by this miracle there are very close likenesses between the Original and the copy, the living model and the painting."[51]

In 1756 Miguel Cabrera, the most famous colonial artist of the day, also examined the tilma and reported:

"I believe that the most talented and careful painter if he sets himself to copy this Sacred Image on a canvas of this poor quality, without using sizing, and attempting to imitate the four media employed, would at last after great and wearisome travail, admit that he had not succeeded. And this can be clearly verified in the numerous copies that have been made with the benefit of varnish, on the most carefully prepared canvases, and using only one medium, oil, which offers the greatest facility; and of these, I am clearly persuaded, that *until now there has not been one which is a perfect reproduction - as the best, placed beside the original, evidently shows."*[52]

Cabrera knows whereof he speaks, for his own copy of Our Lady of Guadalupe is considered the most faithful to the original. It was at the dramatic unrolling of this canvas that Pope Benedict XIV exclaimed, *Non fecit taliter omni nationi.* "Not with every nation has he dealt thus."

In 1979 in the tradition of Miguel Cabrera, Dr. Philip Serna Callahan, a biophysicist at the University of Florida, an expert in infra-red photography, and himself a painter, was allowed to examine and photograph the Image. Callahan, a devout Catholic, after setting up his infra-red equipment on a platform, asked for and obtained permission to receive Holy Communion before he began photographing. Concerning the utility of infra-red photography in the study of the holy Image, Callahan writes:

"Infrared photography is recommended before any restoration or cleaning is attempted on old paintings. It is most important because one can often detect undersketching accomplished before the artist applied paint to the canvas. Infrared photography also enables one to determine the nature of the sizing under the paint, provided the layers are not too thick. No study of art work can be considered as complete until the techniques of infrared photography have been utilized, and certainly no valid scientific study is complete without such an analysis."[53]

Callahan who also has a background in entomology makes the interesting comment, that some of the effects of the painting are impossible to accomplish by human hands, but are found in Nature in bird feathers, insects, etc.:

"It is a simple fact that if one stands close to the painting the face is very disappointing as far as depth and coloring are concerned. At a distance of six or seven feet, however, the skin tone becomes what might best be termed Indian-olive (gray-green) in tone. It appears that somehow the gray and 'caked' looking white pigment of the face and hands combines with the rough surface of the unsized tilma to 'collect' light and diffract from afar the olive-skinned hue. Such a technique would be an impossible accomplishment by human hands. It often occurs in nature, however, in the coloring of bird feathers and

butterfly scales, and on the elytra of brightly colored beetles. Such colors are physically diffracted colors and do not depend upon absorption and reflection from molecular pigments but rather on the surface-sculpturing of feathers or butterfly scales. The same physical effect is quite evident in the face and is easily observed by slowly backing away from the painting until the details of the imperfections in the tilma fabric are no longer visible. At a distance where the pigment and surface sculpturing blend together, the overwhelming beauty of the olive-colored Madonna emerges as if by magic. The expression suddenly appears reverent yet joyous, Indian yet European, olive-skinned yet white of hue. The feeling is that of a face as rugged as the deserts of Mexico, yet gentle as a maiden on her wedding night. It is a face that intermingles the Christianity of Byzantine Europe with the overpowering naturalism of New World-Indian. A fitting symbol for all the peoples of a great continent!"[54]

It has been known for some time that there have been some additions to the Image and that these are beginning to flake off, much to the delight of the Catholic Modernists. But Callahan concludes that the original Image cannot be explained in natural terms:

"The original figure, including the rose robe, blue mantle, hands and face...is inexplicable. In terms of this infrared study, there is no way to explain either the kind of color luminosity and brightness of pigments over the centuries. Furthermore, when consideration is given to the fact that there is no underdrawing, sizing, or over-varnish, and the weave of the fabric is itself utilized to give portrait depth, no explanation of the portrait is possible by infrared techniques. It is remarkable that after more than four centuries there is no fading or cracking of the original figure on any portion of the agave tilma, which - being unsized - should have deteriorated centuries ago.

"Some time after the original image was formed, the moon and the tassel were added by human hands, perhaps for some symbolic reason since the moon was important to both Moorish-Spanish and Aztec mythologies.

"Sometime after the tassel and the moon were added, the gold and black line decorations, angel, Aztec fold of the robe, sunburst, stars and background were painted, probably during the 17th century. The additions were by human hands and impart a Spanish Gothic motif to the painting. In all probability, at the same time the tilma

was mounted on a solid support, the orange coloring of the sunburst and white fresco were added to the background. The entire tilma for the first time was completely covered with paint. It seems unlikely that Juan Diego could have worn a tilma stiffened with fresco on the fabric to the Bishop's palace. Therefore, the original must have been the simple figure on the cloth...

"It is known that during the great flood of 1629 the Holy Portrait was taken from the Hermitage chapel by canoe to the cathedral in Mexico City, and that His Excellency Archbishop Don Francisco de Manzoyzuniga promised not to return the Virgin to the Hermitage until he could take her back with 'dry feet'...The Image was returned in 1634...

"In all probability the Holy Image, especially at the bottom and around the edges, suffered some water damage, and the angel and other decorations, as well as the outer fresco white, were added to cover up the damage. This is in no way different from the patches added to the Shroud of Turin to cover the fire damage to the Holy Relic."[55]

Callahan's conclusions regarding extensive human additions to the tilma might well be true, but I suspect he is overdoing it. But his suggestion of a 17th century date for most of them can't possibly be true. In 1570 just 39 years after the apparition, Archbishop Montufar sent King Philip II of Spain a copy of the miraculous Image which was placed in the flag ship of Admiral Andrea Doria in anticipation of the Battle of Lepanto. "The miraculous image of Guadalupe was probably the particular instrument of Mary's presence there as the Warrior Queen and the Immaculate Mother of the Church, the Woman who crushes the head of the serpent."[56] This copy is now enshrined in the Church of San Stephano in Aveto, Italy. It is reproduced in *A Handbook on Guadalupe* (p.95) and is identical to the original, which means that any additions must have been made well before 1570.

The *Codex Saville*, called the "oldest book in America," is an Indian calendar in picture writing that was begun around 1407 and ends around 1540. It is reproduced to size in an overleaf of the *Historical Records and Studies*, Volume XIX, September 1929 of the United States Catholic Historical Society. It is about three and a half feet long with small paintings illustrating important events. Reading from the bottom up, just above the symbol for 1532 is a tiny figure of Our Lady of

Guadalupe about an inch high. The codex was probably kept up to date year after year by Indian scribes and the tiny figure of Our Lady entered in 1531, the year of the apparition. Demarest and Taylor describe it in *The Dark Virgin:*

"Under magnification the tiny figure of the Virgin is startling similar to that in the Holy Portrait. The position in which she stands, her manner of dress, the way she holds her hands in prayer, are the same; the colors are the same in tone, and figure is surrounded by clouds bordering the rays of the sun indicated by thin streaks of yellow. When one considers that this miniature is painted on a very rough, thin, fibrous paper, it is astonishing that the likeness is so closely achieved...It is obviously intended as a figure of the Virgin...as above her head there is a great crown, and there are the clouds and sun rays."[57]

We can see from the *Saville Codex* that the Image was not just a simple figure originally, as Doctor Callahan suggests, but from the first there were clouds and the rays of the sun, and evidently the tilma was completely covered with color from the very beginning. It is possible that on top of these miraculous colors, additions could be made without sizing, but being unvarnished, are now beginning to flake off. I suspect that all the additions were made almost immediately by Indian artists to enhance the pictogram nature of the Image. Doctor Callahan concludes his study:

"The additions to the Image of the Virgin, although by no means technically elegant compared with the original image, nevertheless add a human element that is both charming and edifying. Any single addition - whether moon, Aztec fold, gold and black border, angel or whatever - does not alone enhance the portrait. Taken together, however, the effect is overwhelming. As by magic, the decorations accentuate the beauty of the original and elegantly -rendered Virgin Mary. It is as if God and man had worked jointly to create a masterpiece."[58]

But probably the most tender motherly aspect of the miraculous Image, and so characteristic of Our Lady, is that the reflection of her beloved Juan Diego can still be seen in her eyes:

"Meanwhile, the 'Immortal Ambassador of Holy Mary of Guadalupe' rests content and happy in the beatific vision, close to the Queen who used to call him endearingly her xocoyote and promised

him a great reward. And here at her shrine in Mexico City; for, as recently discovered, the image of Juan Diego is in the pupils of the Virgin's eyes in her miraculous portrait. She wished to keep imprisoned forever in her eyes her beloved Juanito as a precious remembrance of her last visit with him on earth.

"The image discovered in the eyes of the Virgin on her sacred portrait is the bust of a man with a beard and heavy shock of hair, his right arm slightly extended, and his gaze directed straight ahead...The image cannot be that of Bishop Zumárraga, since he was bald and the image shows a full head of hair. The face as seen in the reflected image is remarkably like that of Juan Diego as he is portrayed in the old paintings that are marked with the inscription 'True Portrait.'"[59]

The much maligned (by Lafaye) Fr. Miguel Sanchez who wrote the first Spanish account of the apparitions said:

"When he reached the summit, he found there a beautiful garden of roses of Castile, fresh, fragrant, and with dew upon them; and, holding his mantle, or tilma, in the way the Indians are accustomed to do, he cut as many roses as he could hold in it, and took them into the presence of the Virgin Mary, who was waiting for him at the foot of a tree...And here was the place, without doubt, where the miraculous painting of the blessed Image took place; because the Indian, kneeling in the presence of the Virgin Mary, showed her the roses he had cut, and Our Lady gathering them all into her hands, put them back again into the Indian's mantle."[60]

So it was probably as Juan Diego was kneeling before Our Lady as she was rearranging the roses, that she miraculously imprinted her Image on his tilma, including his reflection in her eyes as she saw him then. This remarkable discovery has been examined by many opthalmologists including Dr. Javier Torella-Bueno. Jody Brant Smith, a non-Catholic who arranged Doctor Callahan's infra-red studies, writes:

"Before I could understand the importance of his discovery I needed to learn something about the physiology of the human eye, in particular what is called the Purkinje-Sanson principle (named after Jan Evangelista Purkinje, Czech physiologist, and Louis Joseph Sanson, French physician, who independently described the phenomenon). In its simplest form, the Purkinje-Sanson law states that whenever we see any object, the object is reflected in each eye, not once but in three different places. This threefold reflection is caused by the curvature of the

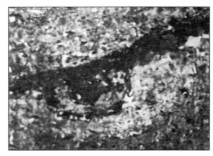

Left: The image of Juan Diego reflected in the eye of Our Lady of Guadalupe similar to an early painting of the seer.

eye's cornea. Two of the reflections are always right side up and one is a always upside down. Depending on the angle at which the object is seen, the three reflections occur on different parts of the eye, because of the differing angles of curvature of the cornea. The curvature also causes the reflected images to be distorted in varying degree.

"On May 26, 1956, Dr. Toroella sent the following letter to Carlos Salinas:

'If we take a light source and put it in front of the eye...we see the cornea, the only part of the eye which can reflect an image in three places [images of Purkinje-Sanson]: the front surface of the cornea, and both front and rear of the lens surfaces, immediately behind...The image of the Virgin of Guadalupe, which has been given to me for study, contains in the cornea these reflections...In the images in question, there is a perfect collocation in agreement with this [principle], the distortion of the figures even concurring with the predicted curvature of the cornea.'"[61]

Brother Eymard reports on an additional examination by Dr. Rafael Torija -Lavoignet:

"It is impossible to attribute to chance, to a textile accident or the pictorial matter this extraordinary coincidence between the localization of the reflections in the Virgin's eyes and the most elaborate and up-to-date laws of optical physiology, especially as it seems that these three reflections code a different focal distance. It is their most amazing property revealed by an experiment made by Doctor Lavoignet. If the light of an opthalmoscope, set with a suitable lens, is directed onto the reflection corresponding to Purkinje No. 2, the reflection fills with

light and 'shines like a little diamond.' Now the same result is achieved with the third reflection provided the lens is changed...Each of these reflections, therefore, has recorded the focal distances of the two faces of the crystalline, and the 'painted' eye on a flat opaque surface reacts in the

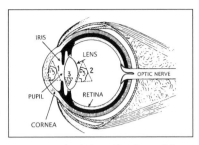

Diagram of triple reflection of Juan Diego in the eye of the sacred Image.

presence of light as though it were a living eye. Mysteriously, the light enters onto 'the depth,' which explains, moreover, the phenomenon mentioned above: when Lavoignet aims the light of the apparatus - as though to inspect the back of the eye - the eye lights up and the iris becomes brilliant."[62]

Let me finally conclude this little study of Our Lady of Guadalupe with a touching personal story by Father Rahm which occurred before the reflections in Our Lady's eyes became generally known:

"On December 8, 1957, I was preaching a Holy Hour sermon on Our Lady at Sacred Heart Church, El Paso, Texas. At the conclusion of the sermon, by some sort of rhetoric, I decided on the spur of the moment to end my words in the following fashion. I told the parishioners how, when I was a child, my mother lifted me close to her eyes, saying: 'Son, see how much I love you; you are reflected in my eyes.' Being a child, I was quite surprised to see my image in my mother's own eyes. I understood how much my mother loved me and have never forgotten this impressive incident.

"After having told this little story, I continued: 'Now let us always live as if we are reflected in Our Lady's eyes.'"[63]

References

1. Carlos de Sigüenza y Góngora, Primavera Indiana, Mexico City, 1945, p.31; quoted in: Jacques Lafaye, *Quetzalcoatl and Guadalupe: The Formation of Mexican National Consciousness 1531-1813*, University of Chicago Press, 1976, p. 63.

2. Fr. George Ring, S.J., *The Gods of the Gentiles*, Bruce Publishing Company, Milwaukee, 1938, p. 196.

3. Bro. Herbert F. Leies, S.M. *Mother for a New World: Our Lady of Guadalupe*, The Newman Press, Westminster, MD, 1964, pp. 18, 19.

4. Bro. Bruno Bonnet-Eymard, "Our Lady of Guadalupe and Her Wonderful Image in the Light of Science and History," *The Catholic Counter-Reformation in the XXth Century*, No. 127, Morden, Surrey, England, October 1980, pp. 26, 46.

5. Bonnet-Eymard, *op. cit.*, p. 28. The human sacrifices offered in pagan Greece and Rome were pale in comparison to those offered in Mexico, but St. Clement of Alexandria (d. 217) cried out in protest:

   "...Philanthropic, assuredly, the demons appear, from these examples; and how shall those who revere the demons not be corresponding pious? The former are called by the fair name of saviours; and the latter ask for safety from those who plot against their safety, imagining that they sacrifice with good omens to them, and forget that they themselves are slaying men. For a murder does not become sacrifice by being committed in a particular spot. You are not to call it a sacred sacrifice, if one slays a man either at the altar or on the highway to Artemis or Zeus, any more than if he slew him for anger or covetousness, - other demons very like the former; but a sacrifice of this kind is murder and human butchery...

   "But though you perceive and understand demons to be deadly and wicked, plotters, haters of the human race, and destroyers, why do you not turn out of their way, or turn them out of yours? What truth can the wicked tell, or what good can they do any one?"

   St. Clement of Alexandria, *Exhortation to the Heathen, The Ante-Nicene Fathers*, Volume II, Edited by Rev. Charles Roberts, D.D., and James Donaldson, L.L.D., Charles Scribners Sons, New York, 1926, p. 183.

   St. Thomas Aquinas far removed from pagan idolatry is able to write more objectively than St. Clement, but he comes to the same conclusions:

"...Idolatry had a twofold cause. One was a dispositive cause; this was on the part of man, and in three ways. First, on account of his inordinate affections, forasmuch as he gave other men divine honor, through either loving or revering them too much. This cause is assigned (Wis. xiv. 15): 'A father being afflicted with bitter grief, made to himself the image of his son, who was quickly taken away: and him who then had died as a man he began now to worship as a god.' The same passage goes on to say (verse 21) that 'men serving either their affection, or their kings, gave the incommunicable name' (Vulg., -"names"), i.e. of the Godhead, 'to stones and wood.' Secondly, because man takes a natural pleasure in representations, as the Philosopher observes (Poet. 4), fashioned by the diligence of the craftsman, he gave them divine worship; hence it is written (Wis. 13: 11-17): 'If an artist, a carpenter, hath cut down a tree, proper for his use, in the wood...and by the skill of his art fashioneth it, and maketh prayer to it, inquiring concerning his substance, and his children, or his marriage.' Thirdly, on account of their ignorance of the true God, inasmuch as through failing to consider His excellence men gave divine worship to certain creatures on account of their beauty or power, wherefore it is written (Wis. 13: 1, 2): 'All men...neither by attending to the works have acknowledged who was the workman, but have imagined either the fire, or the wind, or the swift air, or the circle of the stars, or the great water, or the sun and the moon to be the gods that rule the world.'

"The other cause of idolatry was completive, and this was on the part of the demons, who offered themselves to be worshipped by men, by giving answers in the idols, and doing things which to men seemed marvelous. Hence it is written (Ps. xcv, 5): 'All the gods of the Gentiles are devils.'" Summa Theologica, II-II, Q. 94, a. 4.

6. Jonathan Norton Leonard, *Ancient America*, Time-Life Books, Alexandria, Virginia, 1967, p. 59.

7. Dr. Charles Wahlig, "Juan Diego Ambassador of the Queen of Heaven," *A Handbook on Guadalupe*, Franciscan Marytown Press, Libertyville, IL, 1974, pp. 48, 49.

8. Warren H. Carroll, *Our Lady of Guadalupe and the Conquest of Darkness*, Christendom Publications, Front Royal, Virginia, 1983, pp. 19, 20.

9. *A Handbook on Guadalupe*, op. cit., p. 71.

10. All Quotes from Our Lady are from the *Nichan Mophua*, written in Nahuatl, the language of the Aztecs, by the famous Indian convert Don Antonio Valeriano, a relative of Montezuma, who knew Juan Diego personally.

11. Sr. Simone Watson, O.S.B., *The Cult of Our Lady of Guadalupe*, The Liturgical Press, Collegeville, MN, 1964, p. 70.

12. *A Handbook on Guadalupe*, pp. 147, 148.

13. Leies, *op. cit.*, p. 58.

14. Fr. Harold J. Rahm, S.J., *Am I not Here*, Ave Maria Institute, Washington, NJ, 1961, pp. 121, 122.

It would be too much of a digression in the body of this article to go into the ramifications of Father Rahm's point regarding the necessity of the Church for salvation, but just let me make a few remarks in this footnote. Jacques Lafaye, probably the most sinister of the current crop of anti-apparitionists, tries to make a big case out of what he calls the "spiritual problem" of the Indians, that is whether or not they could be considered human. How could they be descended from Adam and Eve? But this is strictly a non-problem. It is true that there were a few armchair theologians in the universities back in Europe who speculated that the Indians were pre-Adamites, or survivors of the race of Cain who had escaped the Deluge, etc., but from the very beginning, Ferdinand and Isabella had no doubt that the Indians were indeed descendants of Adam and Eve, and that it was their Christian duty to evangelize them, and they soon had Papal Briefs to encourage them. Nor was it ever a problem to the missionaries in the field, the famous "Twelve Apostles" of the Franciscans.

But there was indeed a "spiritual problem" concerning the Indians that Lafaye never seems to have heard of, that has continued down to our own day, the problem of invincible ignorance. St. Thomas Aquinas taught that explicit faith in the Incarnation (II-II, Q. 2, a.7) and in the Blessed Trinity (II-II, Q. 2, a. 8) was absolutely necessary for salvation, but since the pre-Columbian Indians were invincibly ignorant of these truths of the faith, some theologians, especially the Franciscan Andreas De Vega (d. 1560) speculated that a pre-Columbian Indian of good will could have been saved without explicit faith in the Incarnation and the Trinity (Cf. Address to the Confraternity of Catholic Clergy, Third National Colloquium, November 1977, by Fr. Peter Finnegan, O.P., "The Priest the Word of God and the Magisterium," Cardinal Communications, New London, CN).

But this opinion of De Vega was not shared by the majority of the theologians of his time. For example, the great Jesuit theologian, Francisco Suarez (d. 1617) taught concerning a person of good will involved in invincible ignorance, "Whoever has not set up obstacles against it will receive the light or the call...either externally by means of men...or by an interior illumination by means of angels" *(De Praedestinatione et Reprobatione, 1. IV, c. 3, n. 19, quoted in Fr. Ricardo Lombardi, S.J., The Salvation of Unbelievers, p.232).* This is of course exactly what happened in the case of the king of Texcoco, Nezahualcoyotl and his son Nezahuapilli, and Montezuma's sister, the princess Papantzin.

This opinion of De Vega was also rejected by the Magisterium as well. In 1679 Pope Innocent XI condemned a proposition which implied that one could be justified without supernatural faith or revelation: "A faith amply indicated from the testimony of creation, or from a similar motive, suffices for justification" (Denz. 2123). Finally in 1703 during the reign of Pope Clement XI when the missionary movement to the Amerindians was at its height, the Holy Office responded to an inquiry from the Bishop of Quebec:

"Question. *Whether it is possible for a crude an uneducated adult, as it might be with a barbarian, to be baptized, if there were given to him only an understanding of God and some of His attributes, especially His justice in rewarding and punishing, according to this remark of the Apostle: 'He that cometh to God must believe that He is, and that He is a rewarder' (11:16), from which it is to be inferred that a barbarian adult, in a certain case of urgent necessity, can be baptized even though he does not explicitly believe in Jesus Christ.*

"Response. *A missionary should not baptize one who does not explicitly believe in the Lord Jesus Christ, but is bound to instruct him about all those matters which are necessary, by a necessity of means, in accordance with the capacity of the one to be baptized "(Denz. 2380).*

To an additional inquiry the Holy Office responded, that even an adult Indian at the point of death, must make an act of

Mexican pilgrims inspire admiration by their simple faith and penances.

faith in the Trinity and the Incarnation before he could be baptized (Denz. 2381).

It is indeed a great mystery why, in the Providence of God, the evangelization of the Amerindians was delayed for so long. In the *Acts of the Apostles* (16:7,8) we read that the Holy Spirit forbade St. Paul to preach in Asia, but rather urged him to cross over into Macedonia. God's reasons for His actions will only be revealed at the Last Judgment, but perhaps we can gain a hint of them by the following outstanding fact:

"Perhaps it was no mere coincidence that, in the year that Martin Luther was born in Eisleben, Saxony, Hernan Cortes first saw the light of day in Medellin, Spain. But, could it have been another pure coincidence that Luther posted his protest against the Church in 1519, the very year that witnessed the embarking of Cortes for his conquest of Mexico to bring Christianity to a new people? The light of faith rejected on one side of the Atlantic would be offered to those in the darkness of heathenism on the other side. Hernan Cortes would serve as an advance-guard to free a people tied with loathsome fetters of snake-worship and of human sacrifice. His would be a mission of deliverance from captivity, achieved through war and the overthrow of a pagan empire. And, when peace would settle on the new land, there would be the fruitful apparition of the Mother of God to warm the hearts of the people to the acceptance of her Divine Son. This would be the day of salvation, and Cortes was chosen to 'prepare the way' for its realization. (Leies, op. cit., p.25)"

15. Rahm, *op. cit.*, p. 56.

16. *Idem*, p. 57.

17. *Nichan Mopuha, A Handbook on Guadalupe*, pp. 156, 157.

18. *La Siempre Virgen Maria de Guadalupe*, Folleto, E.V.C. No. 410 (*El Verdadero Catolicismo, 1953*), p. 15; Quoted in Donald Demarest and Coley Taylor, *The Dark Virgin*, Coley Taylor Inc. Publishers, New York, 1956, p. 27.

19. Fr. P. Mariano Cuevas, S.J., *Album Historico Guadalupano del IV CENTENARIO* (Mexico, D.F.: Escuela Tipographica Salesiana, 1930, pp. 21, 22; quoted in Rahm, *Op. cit.*, pp. 87, 88.

20. *A Handbook on Guadalupe*, p. 138.

21. Fr. José A. Romero, S.J., Breve Historia de las Apariciones, p. 88; quoted in Leies, *op. cit.*, p. 386.

22. Leies, *op. cit.*, p. 394.

23. *Idem*, p. 78.

24. *Idem* p. 166.

25. Lafaye, *op. cit.*, p. 296.
26. *Idem*, p. 214.
27. *Idem*, pp. 186, 187.
28. Joseph Campbell, *The Power of Myth:* with Bill Moyers, Doubleday, New York, 1988, pp. 148, 22.
29. D. Scott Rogo, *Miracles: A Parascientific Inquiry Into Wondrous Phenomena*, Dial Press, New York, 1982, p. 9.
30. Rogo, *op. cit.*, p. 305.
31. *Idem*, p. 308.
32. *Idem*, pp. 211-213.
33. Quoted in Jacques Monod, *Chance and Necessity*, translated from the French by Austryn Wainhouse, Vintage Books, Random House, New York, 1971, p. 138.

In an article which appeared in *Fidelity* magazine, Edward O'Brien Jr. complains against Rogo in almost the identical words of Mauriac:

> *"Isn't it generally easier to believe in miracles than to believe in Rogo's poltergeist? Rogo is asking us to believe that man can create independently existing entities. Perhaps it is less credulous to believe that God makes strange things happen from time to time."*

"Take That Ripley: Everything You Wanted to Know about Miracles...But Were Afraid to Ask," *Fidelity*, Notre Dame, IN, February, 1989, p. 23.

34. Rogo, pp. 217, 218
35. Lafaye, p. 298.
36. Lauren van der Post, *Jung and the Story of Our Time*, Pantheon Books, Random House, New York, 1975, p. 213.
37. John Dart, *The Laughing Savior, The Discovery and Significance of the Nag Hammadi Gnostic Library*, Harper and Row, New York, 1976, pp. 32, 33.
38. Edward F. Edinger, *Ego and Archetype*, Penguin Books, New York, 1972, pp. 19, 21.

Lest there be any doubt about the similarity of the treatment of the serpent in Gnosticism and Jungian psychology, let me give one more illustration. Here again is Joseph Campbell.

> *"The power of life causes the snake to shed its skin, just as the moon sheds its shadow. The serpent sheds its skin to be born again, as the moon its shadow to be born again. They are equivalent symbols. Sometimes the*

serpent is represented as a circle eating its own tail. That's an image of life. Life sheds one generation after another to be born again. The serpent represents immortal energy and consciousness engaged in the field of time, constantly throwing off death and being born again. There is something tremendously terrifying about life when you look at it that way. And so the serpent carries in itself the sense of both fascination and the terror of life.

"Furthermore, the serpent represents the primary function of life, mainly eating. Life consists in eating other creatures. You don't think about that very much when you make a nice-looking meal. But what you are doing is eating something that was recently alive. And when you look at the beauty of nature, and you see the birds picking around -they're eating things. You see the cows grazing, they're eating things. The serpent is a traveling alimentary canal, that's about all it is. And it gives that primary sense of shock, life in its most primal quality. There is no arguing with that animal at all. Life lives by killing and eating itself, casting off death and being reborn, like the moon. This is one of the mysteries that these symbolic, paradoxical forms try to represent.

"Now the snake in most cultures is given a positive interpretation. In India, even the most poisonous snake, the cobra, is a sacred animal, and the mythological Serpent King is the next thing to the Buddha.

"The serpent represents the power of life engaged in the field of time, and of death, yet eternally alive. The world is but its shadow - the falling skin. The serpent was revered in the American Indian traditions, too. The serpent was thought of as a very important power to be made friends with. Go down to the pueblos, for example, and watch the snake dance of the Hopi, where they take the snakes in their mouths to make friends with them and then send them back to the hills. The snakes are sent back to carry the human message to the hills, just as they have brought the message of the hills to the humans. The interplay of man and nature is illustrated in this relationship with the serpent. A serpent flows like water and so is watery, but its tongue continually flashes fire. So you have the pairs of opposites together in the serpent.

'MOYERS: In the Christian story the serpent is the seducer.

'CAMPBELL: That amounts to a refusal to affirm life. In the biblical tradition we have inherited, life is corrupt, and every natural impulse is sinful unless it has been circumcised or baptized. The serpent was the one who brought sin into the world. And the woman was the one who handed the apple to man. This identification of the woman with sin, of the serpent with sin, and thus of life with sin, is the twist that has been given to the whole story in the biblical myth and doctrine of the Fall.'"

Campbell, pp. 45, 46.

A pyramid with the fierce looking snake god. Atop these pyramids many thousands of humans were sacrificed to their demon gods. Their hearts were torn out and their bodies were rolled down the sides of the pyramids.

39. The Ante-Nicene Fathers, Volume I, Irenaeus *Against Heresies*, edited by Rev. Alexander Roberts, D.D. and James Donaldson, The Christian Literature Publishing Company, Buffalo, 1885, p. 415.

40. Fr. Wilhelm Schmidt, S.V.D., *Primitive Revelation*, translated by Rev. Joseph J. Baierl, S.T.D., B. Herder Book Co., St. Louis, 1939, p. 149.

41. Fr. Wilhelm Schmidt, S.V.D., *The Origin and Growth of Religion*, translated by H.J. Rose, The Dial Press, New York, 1931, pp. 262, 263.

Let me give just one illustration of an actual field report to prove that the most primitive peoples do not have the "primordial male-female dualism" of Jung and Lafaye. This is by another Society of the Divine Word Father, Wilhelm Koppers.

"From Bambuti (Pygmy) reports and myths we can reconstruct man's beginnings along the following lines: After God had created the world and man, he dwelt among them. He called them his children. They gave him the name of father. He had created, not begotten them, for no female deity is ever mentioned in connection with him. He showed himself a good father to men for he so placed them in this world that they could live without much effort and were above all free from care and fear. Neither elements nor animals were inimical to man and food stuffs grew ready to his hand. In short, the world was a paradise as long as God dwelt among men. He was not visible to them but he was in their midst and spoke to them.

"The 'paradise' in which God first placed man was the primeval forest. He put it at man's disposal together with all that it produced. God had, however, also given one commandment on the keeping of which man's fate depended. He had threatened the severest punishment if man should disobey. The whole of creation would enter into league against the rebellious subject. Animals, plants and elements, which had so far been man's friends and servants, would then become his enemies. Toil and misery, sickness and death would follow in the wake of his rebellion. Most painful of all, God would withdraw from man and depart. In spite of these threats and warnings the first man failed to stand the test. He disobeyed and was immediately made to feel the consequences of his sin. What caused him the most suffering was God's departure. God disappeared. He withdrew and was no longer perceptible. He is not dead, the Bambuti say; if he were his bones would have been found. He has withdrawn up the river, to higher regions...In the opinion of the Pygmies who spoke of these things, God's withdrawal was undoubtedly the greatest catastrophe that ever befell mankind; the other consequences of sin were less keenly felt. Thus ended the first act in the history of mankind."

Fr. Wilhelm Koppers, S.V.D., *Primitive Man and His World Picture*, translated by Edith Raybould, Sheed and Ward, New York, 1952, pp. 43, 44.

42. Campbell, *op. cit.*, pp. 51, 52.

43. Lafaye, *op. cit.*, pp. 310, 311.

Chesterton would have called this final peroration of Lafaye: *"The little hiss that only comes from hell."*

"A Party Question," *The Queen of the Seven Swords*, Sheed and Ward, London, 1926, p. 13.

44. Rahm, *op. cit.*, pp. 89, 90.

45. *Idem*, pp. 26, 28.

46. *Idem*, p. 104.

47. Leies, *op. cit.*, p. 26.

48. Rahm, *op. cit.*, p. 26.

49. Andrew Lang, *The Making of Religion*, (1912) AMS Press, New York, 1968, pp. 17, 18.

50. Gilbert K. Chesterton, *Orthodoxy*, quoted in Demarest and Taylor, *op. cit.*, p. 29.

51. Demarest and Taylor, *op. cit.*, p. 158.

52. *Idem*, pp.159-161.

53. *Idem*, p.155.

54. Philip Serna Callahan, *The Tilma Under Infra-Red Radiation, CARA Studies on Popular Devotion*, Vol. II, Guadalupan Studies, Center for Applied Research in the Apostolate, Washington, D.C., 1981, p. 5.

55. Callahan, *op. cit.*, p. 15.

56. *Idem*, pp. 18, 19.

57. *A Handbook on Guadalupe* , p. 92, footnote.

58. Demarest and Taylor, *op. cit.*, pp. 176, 177.

59. Callahan, *op. cit.*, p. 19.

60. Leies, *op. cit.*, pp. 133, 135.

61. Demarest and Taylor, p. 109.

62. Jody Brant Smith, *The Image of Guadalupe: Myth or Miracle*, Doubleday and Company, Garden City, New York, 1983, pp. 79, 80.

63. Bonnet-Eymard, *op. cit.*, p. 39.

64. Rahm, *op. cit.*, p. 74.

For Further Reading on Guadalupe

A Handbook on Guadalupe, **recently published (1997) is a treasure-trove of facts and insights and exciting new discoveries about the "continuous miracle" of the Image of Guadalupe.**

Made up of more than 40 concise chapters by leading experts, it's a compendium on Guadalupe.

You'll learn that the over 550 year old image is intact and vivid despite being exposed to candle smoke, heat, acid fumes, kisses and touched by anything from medals to sabers by multitudes for the first 100 years and neither the nitric acid spill (1778) nor the atheist bomb (1921) destroyed it.

You'll learn how the colors are a complete mystery; how the temperature of her image is always 68.6 degrees, regardless of the air temperature; how the stars on Mary's mantle are those that were above Mexico City on the day of the miracle.

You'll discover three reasons why many believe Mary is pregnant; how the colors, flowers, buds, stars on her clothing and other details are actually picture-writing, rich in spiritual meaning for the dejected Indians whom the Spanish conquered.

Plus, you'll read the beautiful theological meaning hidden in each of her maternally tender words; how her Image brought about the conversion of nine million Indians in less than a decade; of the countless miracles Mary's image has wrought, including closing of abortion mills; the great importance of Bl. Juan Diego as patron of the lay apostolate; why Our Lady of Guadalupe is of special importance for North Americans; why Pope John Paul II could've been arrested during his 1979 pilgrimage to Guadalupe. The Handbook's 226 pages have 50 illustrations (20 full color) and the text of the earliest known account, *Nican Mopohua*; and *MUCH* more.

— *Fr. Paul Marx, OSB*

See last page for further details of this and other Academy of the Immaculate Books.

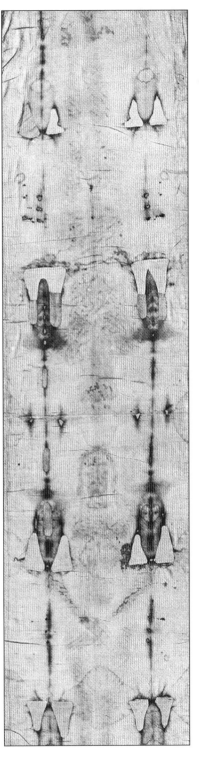

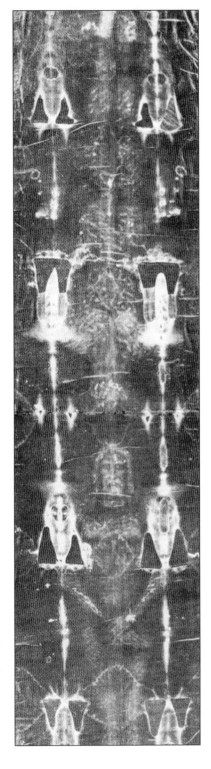

The frontal and dorsal image of the Man on the Shroud as they appear in positive and negative. It wasn't until after photography was discovered in the mid-nineteenth century that the above positive image of the shroud as it normally looks to the human eye was reversed giving us for the first time in 1898 the true image of the crucified Christ as He was laid out on the shroud and tomb

Part II

The Holy Shroud of Turin

The Shroud of Our Lord is mentioned in all three of the Synoptic Gospels:

In Matthew:

"And Joseph taking the body wrapped it up in a clean linen cloth (27:5)."

In Mark:

"And Joseph buying fine linen, and taking him down, wrapped him up in the fine linen (15:46)."

And in Luke:

"And taking him down, he wrapped him in fine linen. (25:53)."

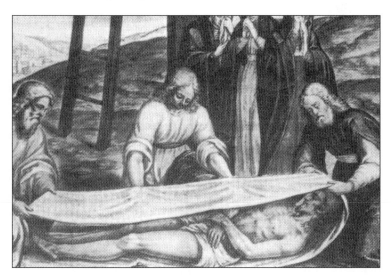

Holy Scripture and the Holy Shroud

The Gospels were inspired in Greek, and the Greek word for "clean linen cloth" or "fine linen" is *sindon*. But the word *sindon* does not appear in the Gospel of John:

"And when he stooped down, he saw the linen cloths lying but yet he went not in. Then cometh Simon Peter, following him, and went into the sepulchre, and saw the linen cloths lying. And the napkin that had been about his head, not lying with the linen cloths, but apart, wrapped up into one place (20:5-7)."

The Greek word for "linen cloths" is *othonia*, and for "napkin" *soudarion*. Scripture scholars have tried to harmonize the Synoptic and the Johannine accounts of Our Lord's burial, some identifying the *sindon* of the Synoptics with the *soudarion* of John, and others with the *othonia*. Fr. Werner Bulst, S.J. in his excelent *The Shroud of Turin*, presents the cases made by various exegetes for both opinions.[1] Some scholars of the *sindon* = *soudarion* ("fine linen" or Shroud = napkin) school, for example Bro. Bruno Bonnet-Eymard, argue from the fact that *soudarion* means "shroud" in Aramaic, the language spoken by St. John.[2] But St. John wrote in Greek, not in Aramaic, and *soudarion* in Greek means " a napkin, or cloth to wipe off sweat" (Lidell and Scott, *Greek-English Lexicon*).

That St. John did not mean "shroud," but "napkin," is clear, I think, from his account of the raising of Lazarus:

"And presently he that had been dead came forth, bound feet and hands with winding bands, and his face was bound with a napkin (John 11:44)."

The word for "napkin" used by St. John is *soudarion*, and I think it is obvious from the context that the *soudarion* is a small head covering and not a shroud. Brother Eymard also suggests that the veil worn by Moses after he had come down from Mount Sinai is a type of Our Lord's *soudarion*/Shroud:

> *"And when Moses came down from Mount Sinai, he held the two tables of the testimony, and he knew not that his face was horned from the conversation of the Lord. And Aaron and the children of Israel seeing the face of Moses horned, were afraid to come near...And having done speaking, he put a veil upon his face (Exodus 34:29, 30, 33)."*

The shining of Moses's face is meant to be type of one of the qualities of Our Lord's glorified body, its brightness or clarity, which was foreshadowed at the Transfiguration on Mount Tabor:

> *"And he was transfigured before them. And his face did shine like the sun: and his garments became white as snow (Matthew 17:2)."*[3]

Hebrew is very close to Aramaic, but the Hebrew word in the Massoretic text in this passage for "veil" is not the Aramaic/Greek *soudarion*, but *mas'veh*, which is translated in the Greek Septuagint by *kaluma*. Brother Eymard suggests that the "veil" went over the head of Moses and fell down to his feet. But it seems more reasonable that this "veil" was a small head covering, similar to the "napkin"/*soudarion* which covered the head of Lazarus, and not a shroud. An additional argument is from the parable of the "pounds": "And another came in saying: Lord, behold here is thy pound, which I have kept laid up in a napkin" (Luke 19:20). Again the Greek word is *soudarion*, indicating a small rather than a large cloth.

Ian Wilson, another Shroud scholar, also supports the *soudarion*/Shroud theory, and believes that it eventually became the Holy Mandylion of Byzantine tradition.[4] The Mandylion is always represented as just a portrait bust of Our Lord, not a full length figure. According to the historian Eusebius of Caesarea (c. 340) a ruler of Edessa, Agbar was given a portrait of Jesus by the Apostle St. Jude, who is often pctured holding this picture. This account is rejected by critical historians, but it might well contain some kernel of truth. Wilson suggests that this picture of Jesus was the *soudarion*/Shroud which had been folded four times and framed to show just a portrait bust of Our Lord, and that this eventually became the Mandylion of Byzantine tradition. It is certainly possible that the Shroud came to be called the Mandylion, but it is not Scriptural to say that the *soudarion*/napkin **is** the *sindon*/Shroud. It is clear from Scripture that we are dealing with three distinct objects, the *sindon*/Shroud, the *soudarion*/napkin and the *othonia*/linen cloths. I would also like to include in this study a fourth holy object which is clear from Tradition, the Veil of Veronica.

If we return to John's account of the raising of Lazarus: "He that had been dead came forth, bound feet and hands with winding bands, (*othonia*) and his face was bound about with a napkin (*soudarion*)." It seems to me that the napkin/soudarion was bound about the head of Lazarus over his shroud.

The *soudarion*/napkin of Our Lord, according to one tradition, is thought to be the Sudarium of Oviedo in Spain. This ancient cloth has no image, but is covered with blood stains. Dr. Alan and Mrs. Mary Whanger, a husband and wife team from the Medical Center of Duke University, have examined this ancient cloth using a remarkable photographic technique developed by Dr. Whanger, and they report a fantastic 130 congruent blood stains between it and the Shroud. It only takes 45 to 60 points to establish the identity or same source of face images in a court of law.[5] This seems conclusive, to me at least, that the Sudarium of Oviedo is the Scriptural *soudarion*/napkin bound over the face of Our Lord.

I would like to insert at this point another holy object that does not appear in Scripture, the Veil of Veronica, but we are absolutely certain of the authenticity of this sacred relic from Tradition. Some scholars reject the "legend" of Veronica, and consider the Veil a late copy of the Shroud. But it is impossible for the Church to be wrong on the Sixth Station of the Cross, "Veronica Wipes the Face of Jesus," and this sacred relic is now kept in St. Peter's, where it has been honored from the early ages of the Church, and is publicly exhibited several times a year.

The Likeness of Christ by the Anglican scholar Thomas Heaphy appeared in 1886, and although he does not believe in the traditional story of St. Veronica nor the acheiropoetic nature of this image, he gives an excellent description of the Veil:

"The picture consists of a life-size head of Our Lord, represented as lying during the three days in the sepulchre, or at all events, at some point of time between the last moment of the crucifixion and the resurrection. The ascertained history of this work reaches back directly to the second century; but, independently of all question of age, it is a production that must stand alone for its extraordinary conception, and the power, indeed, almost inspiration, with which the conception is worked out. Like most others of the same class, it is much obscured, and in many parts nearly obliterated by the decay of the cloth on which it is executed. But the very rags and stains, by dimming its execution, and taking away the appearance of the hand of man, seem to add to its singular impressiveness. The wet, matted hair, the tears, the blood-drops from the crown of thorns, are expressive of the stern reality of death, while the calm, nearly closed eyes, the gently-parted lips, speak not of corruption, but of the spirit at that moment in Paradise, and of the "shortly to be accomplished" resurrection. So replete is this image with concentrated thought and feeling, that it almost forces on us the conviction that unless he that produced it was, in the fullest sense of the term, inspired, he must have seen what he depicted. Like others of the greatest triumphs of Art, this effort has been accomplished with the meanest of instruments: a piece of cloth, without anything in the shape of preparation, a little transparent pigment, apparently nothing more than a stain without color. Nevertheless, this dimly-figured head, on a tattered rag - for its inspiration, its conception and its power of execution - is certainly unsurpassed, perhaps hardly equaled, in the whole range of Art."[6]

The modern devotion to the Veil of Veronica began in 1845 at the Carmel of Tours in France with a series of private revelations to a young nun, Sister Marie de St. Pierre of the Holy Family. In obedience to her superiors Sister Marie recorded these communications:

"There Our Lord vividly portrayed before me the pious and charitable act of Veronica, who, with her veil, had wiped His most Holy Face, covered with spittle, dust, sweat and blood. The Saviour made me understand that, at present, the impious by their blasphemies renewed the outrages and indignities offered His Holy Face...After showing me this, Our Lord Jesus Christ said to me, I seek Veronicas to wipe and honor My Divine Face which has few adorers! By My Holy Face you will work wonders."[7]

In 1849 when Pope Pius IX had been forced to flee to Gaeta during the revolution in Rome, he ordered special public prayers during which a three-day exposition took place in St. Peter's Basilica of the True Wood of the Cross and the Relic of Veronica's Veil. And it was here that an unusual prodigy took place:

"Through another veil of silk which covers the true Relic of Veronica's Veil, and absolutely prevents the features from being distinguished, the Divine Face appeared distinctly, as if living, and was illumined by a soft light; the features assumed a death-like hue, and the eyes, deep-sunken, wore an expression of great pain...this prodigy...lasted three hours."[8]

Soon afterward copies of the true Image of the Holy Face were printed, touched to the True Veil and several reached the Carmel of Tours. Unfortunately Sister Marie de St. Pierre had died in 1848, but the Prioress gave two of these copies to Monsieur Leon Dupont, a pious layman who had been a zealous supporter of Sister Marie de St. Pierre. He hung one of these images in his parlor and kept a lamp burning before it night and day. This soon attracted numerous visitors, and an extraordinary number of conversions and miraculous cures took place. On the death of this "holy man of Tours" in 1876, the bishop, Monseigneur Colet, established a public oratory in Leon Dupont's parlor. Here a Confraternity of the Holy Face was erected, and in 1885 Pope Leo XIII established in this oratory the Archconfraternity of the Holy Face, fulfilling the request which Our Lord had made to Sister Marie de St. Pierre.[9]

I hope I have made a convincing case for the authenticity of Veronica's Veil. It is not a late copy of the Shroud as some scholars claim. After that long digression, I had better recapitulate. We saw that the Shroud is mentioned in all three Synoptic Gospels, and that the Greek word used is *sindon*, translated "fine linen." But in the Gospel of St. John the word *sindon* is not found, but rather two words: *soudarion*, translated "napkin," and othonia, translated "linen cloths." Some scholars identify the *sindon*/Shroud of the Synoptics with the *soudarion*/napkin of John, while others identify the *sindon*/Shroud with the *othonia*/linen cloths. We have just examined the *sindon*/Shroud = the *soudarion*/napkin claim, as represented by Bro. Bruno Bonnet-Eymard and Ian Wilson, and rejected it. Now let us turn to the *sindon*/Shroud = the *othonia*/linen cloths theory.

One such scholar who identifies the *sindon*/Shroud of the Synoptics with the *othonia*/linen cloths of John is Fr. André Feuillet.[10] Father Feuillet argues that while the Vulgate translates *othonia* by *linteamina* ("linen cloths"), in pagan Greek, *othonia* can mean both "bandages" and "sheet." So he identifies the Shroud (sheet) and the linen cloths (bandages) which bound Our Lord's hands and feet, with *othonia* which he prefers to translate by "funerary linens." But I think that this argument is rebutted by the Gospel of St. Luke. We have already seen Luke's description of Our Lord's burial:

"And taking him down, he wrapped him in fine linen (sindon) (25:23)."

But in Luke's description of the Resurrection we read:

"But Peter rising up, ran to the sepulchre, and stooping down, he saw the linen cloths (othonia) laid by themselves (24:12)."

If the *sindon* and the *othonia* are the same, why did St. Luke use one term for the burial of Our Lord, and another for the Resurrection?

Father Feuillet argues that it was an ancient Jewish custom to tie a *soudarion* (napkin) over the head and under the chin of the deceased to keep the mouth closed, and that the lack of markings on the Shroud on the top of Our Lord's head and the sides of His face, seem to confirm the exercise of this custom in His case. But why would the *soudarion*/ napkin be used for this purpose rather than the othonia, the linen cloths which were used to bind Our Lord's hands and feet? These were evidently narrow strips of linen cloth like bandages, and I presume the *soudarion*/napkin was a larger square or oblong piece of linen cloth, not a narrow band, and thus would have been difficult to tie around Our Lord's head. Furthermore if a chin strap was used on the head of Our Lord, the beard would have been pulled up under the chin, which is not the case in the image, indicating that Our Lord's mouth was closed in death, and a chin strap was unnecessary.

Brother Eymard rejects the chin strap theory of the *soudarion*, because for one thing, it destroys his analogy with the veil of Moses. But what purpose did the *soudarion*/napkin serve if it was not a chin strap? I think that Brother Eymard's analogy with the veil of Moses is very apt for the *soudarion*/napkin as he proposes, because the veil of Moses and the napkin of Our Lord were probably about the same size. We saw that Moses's veiling of his face was a type of the resurrection of the body, especially as regards one of the qualities of the glorified body, its clarity or brightness. The binding of the *soudarion* around the head of the deceased then, could have been an act of faith in the resurrection of the body, since it too would one day shine like the face of Moses. But why, as it were, two veils: the *sindon*/Shroud and the *soudarion*/napkin? Possibly this was meant to recall the two veils of the Temple in Jerusalem, an inner veil, the Shroud on which Our Lord left His image, and an outer veil, the napkin on which only blood stains remained (the Sudarium of Oviedo). The Temple was a type of Our Lord's body, concerning which He was falsely accused: "Destroy this temple and in three days I will raise it up" (John 2:19).

Father Bulst after giving both attempts to harmonize the Synoptics with St. John by identifying the *sindon* with the *soudarion*, and then with the *othonia*, offers his own solution, namely that the sindon was not in the empty tomb when St. Peter and St. John inspected it. He suggests that when the guards brought the news of the Resurrection of Our Lord to the Sanhedrin, some member of the High Priest's household inspected the empty tomb and took away the *sindon*/Shroud. He thinks that this hypothesis is supported by the apocryphal Gospel of the Hebrews which states that Jesus gave His *sindon* to a servant of the High Priest as a proof of His Resurrection.

I personally agree with Father Bulst, that the attempts to harmonize the *sindon* of the Synoptics with either the *soudarion* or the *othonia* of John are unconvincing, and the whole point of John's...

"Then cometh Simon Peter, following him, and went into the sepulchre, and saw the linen cloths lying, and the napkin that had

been about his head, not lying with the linen cloths, but apart, wrapped up into one place (John 20:6,7)."

...is that the *sindon*/Shroud of the Synoptics was not there, making it a major witness of the Resurrection of Our Lord.

Imagine Our Lord on Easter Sunday morning. Suddenly His glorified body "shines like the sun," imprinting a negatve image on the Shroud which becomes "white as snow" as in the Transfiguration. He sits up, unbinds the linen cloths tying His hands and Feet. He takes the napkin off His head, carefully folds it, and lays it aside. He is naked save for the Shroud. Only Michaelangelo, as far as I know, dared to portray Our Lord rising from the tomb naked, shocking even the permissive society of the Renaissance. Of course He could have instantly created clothes out of nothing, but this seems unlikely. Is it just an accident or Divine Providence that most artists picture Our Lord rising from the tomb loosely clad in a shining white garment, flung over one shoulder and leaving the wound in His side exposed? (The blood stains on the Shroud and the napkin had been instantly dried up by the clarity of Our Lord's glorified body, and the markings on the Shroud look like a slight scorch.) This garment could only be the Shroud. We seem to get some hint of this in the Gospel of Mark:

"And a certain young man followed him, and having a linen cloth (sindon) *cast about his naked body; and they laid hold on him. But he casting off the linen cloth, fled from them naked (Mark 14:50-52)."*

Thus the empty tomb, the Angels, the napkin/*soudarion* and the linen cloths/*othonia* (*vestes*), all bear witness to the glorious Resurrection of Our Lord. As the Church sings in the Mass of Easter:

"Angelicos testes, sudarium et vestes.
Surrexit Christus spes mea."

But the missing *sindon*/Shroud was saved to become a powerful witness for our own times.

"What better way, if you were a Deity, of regenerating faith in a skeptical age than to leave evidence 2,000 years ago that could only be defined by the technology available in that skeptical age?" – *Kenneth Stevenson, project spokesman*

Science and the Holy Shroud

It was the night of May 28, 1898, and the photographer, Secundo Pia, was in his dark room developing the first photograph ever taken of the Holy Shroud of Turin. To his astonishment and awe a majestic portrait of Jesus Christ appeared on his negative plate. "Pia found himself thinking that he was the first man in 1900 years to gaze on the actual appearance of the body of Christ as He laid in the tomb."[11] Gradually the photographer realized what had happened - if the negative produced a positive picture, it could only mean that the Shroud itself was a photographic negative. The German Jesuit, Fr. Werner Bulst writes:

"Should we not consider the Shroud of Turin as a gift to our century? It was photography that detected for us, in the negative image, the magnificent image of the Lord, latent in the Cloth. Only modern and especially scientific investigation has been able to throw light on this unique and so disputed Relic, and to guarantee its authenticity. For the science conscious man of today, we have opened a new and signally appropriate approach to Jesus Christ."[12]

The astounding news of the "secret" of the Holy Shroud soon began to spread through the medical community, especially at the Sorbonne, where a group of doctors made a detailed study of Pia's negative. One of this group, Yves Delage, a professor of anatomy well known for his agnosticism and his aversion to anything supernatural or miraculous, presented a paper on their findings to the Paris Academy of Science in 1902. The paper caused a furor and the secretary of the Academy, Marcellin Berthelot, refused to publish the lecture in the official proceedings. Delage was warned that he was jeopardizing a distinguished scientific career. He later wrote of this incident:

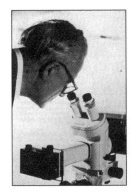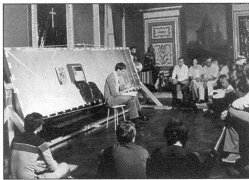

The late Fr. Peter Rinaldi, S.D.B. one of the world's leading authorities on the Holy Shroud. Right: In 1978, a team of over twenty Americans specialists in many fields of scientific research came to Turin to examine the Shroud with the most sophisticated scientific equipment available at that time.

"I willingly recognize that none of these given arguments offer the features of an irrefutable demonstration, but it must be recognized that their whole constitutes a bundle of imposing probabilities, some of which are very near being proven...a religious question has been needlessly injected into a problem which in itself is purely scientific, with the result that feelings have run high, and reason has been led astray. If, instead of Christ, there were question of some person like a Sargon, an Achilles or one of the Pharaohs, no one would have thought of making any objection...I have been faithful to the true spirit of science in treating this question, intent only on the truth, not concerned in the least whether it would affect the interests of any religious party...I recognize Christ as an historical personage and I see no reason why anyone should be scandalized there still exist traces of his earthly life."[13]

As might have been expected, the medical establishment was soon joined in their rejection of the Shroud by the Catholic Modernists. Canon Ulysses Chevalier and the English Jesuit, Herbert Thurston, published a series of documents dating from the fourteenth century which claimed that the Holy Shroud was a forgery. Dr. Pierre Barbet, the author of one of the best books on the Shroud, *A Doctor at Calvary*, summarizes the Modernist case:

"The Shroud at Lirey was...the object of the hostility of the Bish-

ops of Troyes, first of all Henry of Poitiers, and thirty years later Peter d'Arcy, who objected to its being exposed by the canons of Lirey. They complained that the faithful were deserting the relics at Troyes, and were going in large crowds to Lirey. The Charnys [the owners of the Shroud] quickly took back the relic and kept it for thirty years.

"In 1389 they presented their cause to the legate of the new Avignon Pope, and then to the Anti-Pope himself. Both of these authorized the exposition in spite of Peter d'Arcy's prohibition. Then, when the latter complained, Clement VII ended by deciding (a somewhat unworthy solution) that the Bishop could no longer oppose the expositions, but that a declaration should be made at each one that this was a painting representing the true Shroud of Our Lord.

"In the memorandum which he presented to Clement, Peter d'Arcy made grave and malicious accusations of simony against the canons of Lirey. He further claimed that his predecessor had made an inquiry and received the admission of the artist who had painted the Cloth.

"No traces have been ever found of the inquiry or of these avowals; if there was a painter, it is probable that he was the one who copied the Shroud of Lirey to make that of Besançon. The fact is that all the decisions were the result of private interests and were based on the argument that the Gospels were silent in regard to the existence of the markings. It seems that no impartial examination was ever made of the Sheet itself; had this been done, they would have seen, as one can see today, that there is no trace of painting. But the pseudo-Pope Clement VII never seems to have concerned himself with this."[14]

In typical Modernist fashion, Canon Chevalier and Father Thurston had ignored the continuous signs of approval heaped on the Holy Shroud by Popes beginning in the fourteenth century and continuing down to Pope Leo XIII in their own day. Doctor Barbet continues:

"We have seen how the attitude of the anti-Pope Clement VII was as ambiguous as it was obviously political. The hypercritical historian Ulysses seems to attach a special importance to his vacillating opinion, because he believes that this supplies him with an argument against the Shroud, but he might, with more impartiality have balanced this with the constant veneration shown by later legitimate Popes. Once the Shroud had found a home at Chambéry, Paul II attached a collegiate establishment, with twelve canons, to the church where it had been installed by Duke Amadeus IX. Sixtus IV, in 1480 *bestowed on it the name of* Sainte Chapelle. *Julius II, in 1506, granted it a Mass and an Office of its own, for its feast-day which was fixed for May 4th. Leo X extended this feast to the whole of Savoy, and Gregory XIII to Piedmont as well, with the further grant of a plenary indulge to pilgrims.*

"And they all, in their solemn pronouncements, declare that this Shroud is indeed the one in which Jesus was placed in the tomb. They all add that the relics of the Humanity of the Saviour, which it contains, that is to say His Blood, deserve and indeed require to be venerated and adored. This is precisely the cult of latria, *against which the two bishops of Troyes protested which such violence, finally winning the approval of the anti-Pope Clement VII. And this is all the more important, because many decisions taken by the anti-Popes of Avignon were, once the schism was ended, approved by their legitimate Roman successors.*

"It would almost be necessary to mention them all in order to tell of the many marks of veneration which they lavished, and of the indulgences which they granted and confirmed on its behalf. Pius VII solemnly prostrated himself before it in 1814, when he returned in triumph to the Papal States, and Leo XIII showed joy and emotion when he saw the first photograph of the Shroud in 1898."[15]

The Holy Shroud had been under a protective glass covering when Secundo Pia had photographed for the first time in 1898, and the photograph was of relatively poor quality. But in 1931, taking advantage of the tremendous advances that had been made in photography, Giuseppe Enrie was appointed to take a series of photographs of the Shroud without its protective cover. These photographs, which are of superb quality remaining unmatched to this day, launched a whole new era in the medical investigation of the Shroud. Doctor Barbet and other physicians over a period of several years performed a series of somewhat gruesome experiments on severed limbs and cadavers, and even in some cases on themselves and their students, for example, being suspended by their hands, to determine the cause of Our Lord's death.

Let me give just one example from Doctor Barbet's work. In the Gospel of St. John we read: "But one of the soldiers with a spear opened His side, and immediately there came out blood and water. And he that saw it hath given testimony; and his testimony is true. And he knoweth that he saith true; that you may also believe" (John 19:34,35). The historicity of this event was ridiculed by the Higher Critics and their Catholic Modernist disciples. Father Bulst writes:

"For years liberal critics took for granted that this text was any-thing but a historical record of events; in fact it could not be intend-ed as such. At best it was put in rather as a theological opinion, if not even a mere mythological allusion. In support of this the liberals pointed to the 'eloquent silence' of the Synoptics, to the physiological impossibility (sic) of blood and water issuing from a corpse. They like-wise referred to allegedly parallel texts in heathen mythology. They furthermore suggested that the author of the Gospel himself (1 Jn. 5:16) attributed a 'mystical meaning' to the blood and water, etc. R. Bultman finds it ridiculous ('komisch' is the German word he uses) to even consider the physiological possibility of an issue of blood and water, as did Weiss."[16]

In 1907 Pope St. Pius X in his encyclical *Lamentabili* con-demned several Modernist propositions concerning the his-toricity of the Gospel of St. John: "[It is error to say:]

"The narrations of John are not history, in the strict sense but mystical contemplation on the Gospel; the discourses in his Gospel are theological meditations about the mystery of salvation and are devoid of historical truth.

"The fourth Gospel exaggerated the miracles not only to make the extraordinary stand out more clearly but also that they might be more suited to show the work and glory of the Incarnate Word.

"John claims for himself the office of witness to Christ; but in reality he is nothing more than an outstanding witness of Christian life, that is, of the life of Christ in the Church at the end of the first century. (Denz. 2016-2018)."

And here is Doctor Barbet:

"In my first autopsies I noticed that the pericardium always con-tained a quantity of serum (hydropericardium) sufficient for one to see it flowing on the incision of the perietal layer. In some cases it was most abundant.

"I, therefore took my syringe once again, but I pushed the needle very slowly, drawing into the syringe the whole time. I was thus able to feel the resistance of the fibrous pericardium, and as soon as I

perforated it, I drew out a considerable quantity of serum. Then as the needle proceeded on its way, I drew out some blood from the right auricle.

"I then took my knife, and inserting it with the same precautions, I saw the serum flowing and then, as I pressed on, the blood.

"Finally, if one inserts the knife vigorously, a large flow of blood is seen to issue from the wound; but on its edges one can also see that a lesser amount of pericardial fluid is also flowing.

"The water was then pericardial fluid. *And one may imagine that after an exceptionally painful death-agony, as was that of the Saviour, this hydropericardium would have been particularly abundant, so much so that St. John, who was an eye-witness, was able to see both blood and water flowing. He would have imagined that the serum was water. for it has that appearance. As there was no water in the body than the serous fluid, it could not have been pure water. We ourselves use the word hydropericardium, which means the water contained in the pericardium."*[17]

The Holy Shroud then is a magnificent confirmation of the historicity of the Gospels, especially of the Gospel of St. John. Doctor Barbet sums up these years of investigation:

"Let us, then, also study the Shroud, since I started my experiments in order to discover whether its markings correspond with the realities of anatomy and physiology. I undertook this study with a completely open mind, being equally ready to affirm that the Shroud was an absurd fraud, or to recognize its authenticity, but I was gradually forced to agree, on every single point, that its markings were exact. Furthermore, those which seemed the strangest were those which fitted in best with my experiments. The bloodstained pictures were clearly not drawn by the hand of man; they could be nothing but the counter-drawings made by blood which had been previously coagulated on a human body. No artist would have been able to imagine for himself the minute detail of what we now know about the coagulation of blood, but which in the 14th century was unknown. But the fact is that not one of us would be able to produce such pictures without falling into some blunder.

"It was this homogenous group of verifications without one single weak link among them, which decided me, relying on the balance of probabilities, to declare the authenticity of the Shroud, from the point of view of anatomy and physiology, is a scientific fact."[18]

Doctor Barbet published several preliminary studies before his definitive summary, *A Doctor at Calvary*, one of which was entitled *Les Cinq Plaies* ("The Five Wounds"), and about which he tells a beautiful story:

"When I had published the first edition of Les Cinq Plaies, *I went to the École Practique to read it to my old friend, Professor Hovalacque. He was devoted to the subject of anatomy, which he taught to the faculty in Paris, but he was far removed from being a believer. He approved of my experiments and conclusions with growing enthusiasm. When he finished reading he put down my booklet, and he remained silent for a short time in a state of meditation. Then he suddenly burst out with that fine frankness on which our friendship had been built up and exclaimed: 'But then, my friend...Jesus Christ did rise again!' Rarely in my life have I known such deep and happy emotion at this reaction of an unbeliever when faced with a purely scientific work, from which he was drawing incalculable consequences. He died a few months later, and I dare to hope that God rewarded him."*[19]

But why didn't all the doctors believe like Doctor Hovalacque? Around this same time Pope Pius XI gave an allocution to the Pontifical Academy of Science in which he warned scientists:

"May not that terrible vision recur to any of them, that terrible vision which, though for a moment the Apostle of the Gentiles had: namely, that every high intelligence of this kind ought to become deeply interested in the pursuit of the whole truth, so that it might not happen that an intelligence created by God, illuminated by God, would not rise to the Creator. To such an intelligence ought to be applied that great, grave and logical condemnation mentioned by the Apostle himself in these terrible words: 'ita ut sint inexcusabiles' ["so that they are inexcusable"]; as if to say that they could not have an excuse not to have known the Maker, the Creator, after having known His works, His creature."[20]

The Second Vatican Council in its Pastoral Consitution "The Church in the Modern World" (*Gaudium et Spes*) issued in December of 1965, makes an extremely important declaration concerning science and scientists:

"There is no doubt that modern scientific and technical progress

can lead to a certain phenomenism or agnosticism; this happens when scientific methods of investigation, which of themselves are incapable of penetrating to the deepest nature of things, are unjustifiably taken as the supreme norm for arriving at truth. There is a further danger that in this excessive confidence in modern inventions man may think he is sufficient unto himself and give up the search for higher values.

TURIN, Italy, May 24, 1998: The Holy Father praying before the Sacred Shroud which he called an emblem of God's love.

"But these drawbacks are not necessarily due to modern culture and they should not tempt us to overlook its positive values. Among these values we should like to draw attention to the following: study of the sciences and exact fidelity to truth in scientific investigation, the necessity of teamwork in technology, the sense of international solidarity, a growing awareness of the expert's responsibility to help to defend his fellow men, and an eagerness to improve the standard of living of all men, especially of those who are deprived of responsibility or suffer from cultural destitution. All these can afford a certain kind of preparation for the acceptance of the message of the Gospel and can be infused with divine charity by Him Who came to save the world."[21]

So responsible scientific research can be considered, in a certain sense, a "preparation for the Gospel," that is for scientists of good will. For those of bad will it will rather become an additional cause of condemnation. The famous Medical Bureau at Lourdes comes immediately to mind, which is an open invitation to all doctors, believers and unbelievers alike, to examine the authentic, miraculous cures. Some unbelievers are converted, but most are not. The noted French writer, Émile Zola, "was wont to say that he would believe in the miracles of Lourdes did he but see a scratch healed up."[22] This man actually witnessed three miraculous cures, and was not converted, but rather went on to write his mocking and blasphemous novel, *Lourdes*.

Needless to say the Holy Shroud has also had its miracles. At the public exhibition of the Shroud in 1844 "many astonishing miracles were demonstrated to the satisfaction of churchmen. A crippled countess was cured, and became a Sister of Charity. A little girl whose pupil had been cut in two by a scythe was instantly cured; the Bishop of Limburg, where she lived, ordered a solemn procession in thanksgiving for this miracle."[23] But the most famous case occurred in 1955 when a little ten year old English girl, Josephine Wollan, suffering from osteomyelitis, was brought to Turin by a well known English war hero, Leonard Cheshire, a convert and ardent devotee of the Shroud. Josephine was allowed to touch the Shroud, and when asked how she felt, answered simply, "much better thank you."[24] In his book *Shroud* published in 1979, Robert K. Wilcox mentioned that "Josephine survived was in excellent health, married, and with a family of her own."[25]

Little Josephine Wollam's pilgrimage received world wide publicity and many Catholic individuals and groups began petitioning the Cardinal Archbishop of Turin to grant access to the Shroud by qualified scientists to determine its authenticity. Among these was Dr. David Willis, England's foremost medical authority on the Shroud who wrote:

"To carry conviction the investigating experts must be internationally organized and chosen solely for their expertise in the relevant disciplines, quite independently of their nationality or religious persuasions. Truth will only be served if Turin follows the highest traditions of the Lourdes Medical Bureau."[26]

In 1578 St. Charles Borremeo, the Archbishop of Milan, announced that he would make a pilgrimage on foot to Chambry to venerate the Holy Shroud to fulfill a vow he had made during a severe plague in his city. The Duke of Savoy, Immanuel Philibert, the owner of the Shroud, moved it from Chambry to Turin to save the saintly Archbishop the rigors of the mountain journey. St. Charles walked from Milan to Turin in four days, and was welcomed by the thunderous applause of the entire city which had come out to meet him. His feet were bleeding badly, but he resolutely made his way to the Shroud where he was overcome with emotion. To commemorate the 400th anniversary of this event, the Cardinal Archbishop of Turin announced that in 1978 qualified scientists from all over the world would be permitted to inspect and conduct non-destructive tests on the Shroud; the dream come true of Doctor Barbet and many others.

Dr. John Jackson, a professor of physics at the Air Force Academy who had long been interested in the Shroud, began recruiting a team from the very elite of the American high tech establishment. The team eventually numbered forty men and women from places like the Atomic Energy Commission, the Los Alamos Scientific Laboratory, the Pasadena Jet propulsion Laboratory, the Albuquerque Sandia Laboratory, and other such places, and in typical American fashion, called themselves STURP, "Shroud of Turin Research Project."

STURP arrived in Turin with two and a half million dollars worth of laboratory equipment, and were given 120 hours by Church authorities to conduct a whole series of intricate tests. Most of the team members were Protestant and had never been inside a Catholic Cathedral. At the end of their allotted five days "a priest said a prayer, bent and kissed the Shroud. Ernie Brooks, a Presbyterian, waited until he was alone with the Cloth, and he kissed it too."[27]

Years before Doctor Barbet had written:

"It is fully understood that a vigorously scientific proof that these stains are due to blood would require (if they were allowed) physical or chemical examinations; for example, the search by means of the spectroscope for rays of hemoglobin or its derivatives. But, as it has been proved that the other images are not the work of the hand of man, that this Shroud has contained a corpse, can the marks of the wounds which are so rich in details as genuine as they are unexpected, owe their color to anything but blood?"[28]

Back in their laboratory at the Air Force Academy, members of the STURP team led by Dr. John Heller, began testing the mass of data they had accumulated at Turin to determine the chemistry of the Shroud. The French Brother, Bruno Bonnet-Eymard, who was in attendance at the Congress of Turin in 1978, obviously enjoys the high-pressure style of this typically American operation. In a lecture given at the Sorbonne he said:

"It is worth reading [in Heller's Report on the Shroud of Turin*] the account of this amazing improvisation: Heller [Protestant] and Adler [Jewish] spelling out the unpronounceable names of the reagents and books they needed, and the entire Academy coming to life 'as though someone had pushed a magic button: Air Force captains and majors began coming through doors. After writing down two or three names, Jumper and Jackson would tear off the paper and give it to one of the officers, who would take it and exist hurriedly,' and then return with the required chemical products and publications. Heller had asked for xylene in order to extract the microfibres from the adhesive. He was thinking of no more than 'a few ounces.' Suddenly two officers appeared rolling a fifty gallon drum of the stuff!...*

"After twenty-four hours of micro manipulation work under the microscope and the admiring and respectful gaze of the physicists, these were their conclusions:

"...The 'blood' really is blood...It is impossible to quote the whole of this account, which is a delight for chemists without boring the non-scientific reader whom Heller always keeps in sight. What is certain is that each of these tests 'is acceptable in a court of law. Taken together they are irrefutable.'"[29]

In 1981 when the 40 members of STURP held a Symposium in New London, Connecticut, to discuss the results of their investigations, there took place an incident which reminds one of the reaction of the French Academy of Science to the report of Yves Delage in 1902:

"Someone then asked the forty scientists sitting on the stage: 'All who believe this is the authentic Shroud of Christ, raise your hands.' Forty pairs of eyes just stared at him. 'O.K.,' he said, 'all those who don't believe it is authentic raise your hands.' Forty of us sat still; none moved; he was frustrated and hostile."[30]

This is not true science nor the correct scientific method, but a mind set based on the philosophy of empiricism and positivism. These men were not asked to make an act of supernatural faith, but a simple act of reason on which science is based. Are all the converging lines of probability of sufficient weight to indicate that this is the Shroud of Christ? Of course they are! Forty blank stares are not science, but skepticism and agnosticism.

Kenneth E. Stevenson, a former member of STURP who is now a Protestant minister, taught at the Air Force Academy. The Air Force offered him tenure if he would sever his connection with STURP, but disillusioned with the secular humanist environment of the place, he chose to stay with STURP, and severed his connection with the Academy instead. Stevenson believes in the authenticity of the Shroud, and in his excellent book, *The Shroud and The Controversy*, he says that many of the members of STURP will privately admit that the Shroud is authentic, but think that they have to keep up their public agnostic stance for the sake of their "scientific credibility." For instance, he quotes Barrie Schwortz, one of the Jewish members of STURP, as saying:

The arrival of 8,000 lbs. of scientific equipment in Turin for the research project conducted in 1978 by STURP.

"The image on the Shroud matches the account of the crucifixion in the New Testament down to the 'nth degree. Evidence is mounting that the Gospels are quite accurate. This may cause consternation among my family, and other Jewish people, but in my own mind, the Shroud is the piece of cloth which wrapped Jesus after he was crucified."[31]

The Catholic Modernists also claim that to be truly scientific, one has to put faith aside and approach the study of Holy Scripture skeptically. This attitude which is so prevalent among Scripture scholars today, was condemned by

Pope St. Pius X in his encyclical *Lamentabili*: "If an exegete wishes to apply himself profitably to biblical studies, he must first put aside any preconceived opinion about the supernatural origin of Sacred Scripture and interpret it the same as any other merely human document" (Denz. 2012).

Finally the authorities at Turin with the approval of the Pontifical Academy of Science, decided to allow the Shroud to be tested by the Carbon-14 dating method. Catholics should have been warned in advance that this test and other radio metric tests, such as Potassium-Argon, are greatly over-rated. It is by means of these dating methods that some scientists arrive at the tremendous age of the earth which is necessary to support their very shaky theory of evolution, which has become dogma in the secular-humanist establishment. The humanists need these enormous lengths of time for their theory of random mutations to have even a glimmer of scientific respectability. But evolution by random mutations, even given such stretches of time, has been proved to be mathematically impossible.

Creationist scientists, mostly Evangelical Protestants, whose work is almost completely unknown to Catholics, particularly in the area of the Noachian Deluge, clearly demonstrate that the earth is quite young. In the tradition of the French Academy of Science, these findings are ignored by the evolutionist establishment and the Catholic Modernists. For example, the creationist, D. Collins, speaking of Carbon-14 dating, says: "It is not generally appreciated that up to a third of all dates have to be rejected as impossible.[32]

When the results of the Carbon-14 test were announced, supposedly dating the Shroud to the 14th century, there was jubilation in the Catholic Modernist camp. The Catholic John Cornwell who describes the Carbon-14 test as "the test of all tests," writes: "Now that the carbon test points to a medieval date, we can no longer postpone reflecting on the likelihood that the image was an unspeakable product of barbarism manufactured in the interests of ecclesiastical commerce. As we ponder the future implications for the Shroud's religious and moral significance in the light of this appalling possibility."[33]

However new evidence has cast, to put it mildly, considerable doubt on the alleged medieval date claimed by the Carbon-14 testers. These developments are summarized in an article entitled "The Case Is not Closed!" by Stephano M. Paci in the June 1990 issue of *30 Days*:

"*...The new evidence comes principally in two works. One by Brother Bruno Bonnet-Eymard, and was published in France by Les Editions de la Contre-reforme. The second, recently published in Italy, is entitled La Sindone, un enigma alla prova della scienza (The Shroud: An Enigma Faces the Test of Science). The book is co-authored by Orazio Petrosillo, Vatican correspondent for the Rome Il Messagero and Emmanuella Marinelli, Coordinator of an International Center for Documentation on the Shroud.*

"*The evidence the two works present is startling. It suggests that there was a considerable lack of professionalism in the testing process and raises doubts about the validity of the results. These new works present us with mocking and dishonest scientists, with samples of the Shroud which in the research laboratories weighed twice what they weighed when they were cut from the Shroud, with evidence that Carbon-14 tests can be anything but trustworthy. The books argue that the hypothesis of an anti-Catholic conspiracy – an accusation made by Gonella [director of the Vatican Press Office] following the publication of the dating result- now must be viewed with greater attention. 'There are those who speak of a Jewish-masonic conspiracy,' Petrosillo and Marinelli write. Indeed, the Vatican's Secretariat of State has itself opened a dossier to examine whether allegations of such a conspiracy have any basis in fact.*"[34]

The Carbon-14 fiasco was hopefully concluded in August of 1990 when the Vatican announced that it would consider new scientific tests to determine the authenticity of the Shroud. No conditions would be attached to the new tests other than that they should not damage the Shroud. The Vatican spokesman, Joaquin Navaro, described the 1988 results as "strange," and said they conflicted with previous tests, which suggested that the cloth could date back 2000 years. Cardinal Saldarini of Turin announced that the Holy Shroud would again be exposed for public veneration in 1998, implicitly repudiating the Carbon-14 fraud. These developments were given almost no coverage in the secular and Catholic Modernist press.

It seems to have been completely forgotten by both

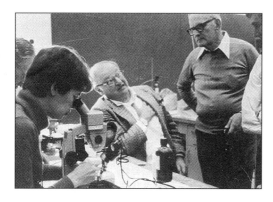

The STURP team after careful analysis established the fact that the blood stains on the Shroud are indeed that of human blood.

Catholic devotees of the Shroud and the investigating scientists, that the date of the Shroud had already been scientifically established, and by a method much more convincing than Carbon-14. As early as 1976, Air Force Captain, John Jackson, asked his friend Bill Mottern, an image enhancement specialist at the Sandia Laboratories in Albuquerque, to place a small three by five slide of the Holy Shroud into a machine called an Interpretation Systems VP-8 Analyzer. To their astonishment, reminiscent of Secundo Pia's, a perfect three dimensional image of Our Lord appeared on the screen. "Finally, Jackson took a deep breath, 'Bill!' he said, 'do you realize that we may be the first people in two thousand years who know exactly how Christ looked in the tomb.'"[35] This three-dimensional effect cannot be achieved by the VP-8 with an ordinary photograph; two photographs separated by a known distance are required, but the Shroud is, of course, no "ordinary photograph."

Jackson also noticed that in the three dimensional image there were strange unnatural bulges over the eyes. In an article on ancient Jewish funeral practices, he discovered that it was a Jewish custom to place small coins on the eyelids of a corpse,[36] which he realized would match the shape of the "bulges" exactly.

"The three dimensional image of the Face does in fact show up on the eyelids two little 'disc-shape' convexes, already observed by Jackson well before the Turin Congress. 'If, for example,' he wrote in a specialist review on the eve of the Turin Congress, 'the disk-shape

images are really coins struck between 29 and 31 years after Christ, would not that then date both the image and the Shroud?' Illustrating this article was a photo already showing a lepton of Pontius Pilate superimposed on the right eyelid; the size and shape corresponded perfectly. Jackson, Jumper and Stevenson, joint authors of the article, even thought they could identify the motif decorating the reverse side of the lepton: an astrologer's staff. But they failed to understand its significance: 'Intriguing points, but to date still inconclusive.'"[37]

But it remained for Fr. Francis Filas, S.J., the author of an excellent book on St. Joseph, *Joseph: The Man Closest to Christ*, to make the crucial discovery:

"In August 1979 almost a year, therefore after the Turin tests, this Jesuit professor at the Loyola University of Chicago (died on 15 February 1985 at the age of 69) deciphered on the right eyelid an imprint of the same size, diameter 15 mm., and of the same cut as a coin struck under Pontius Pilate, bearing an astrologer's staff, the emblem of the superstitious governor. On an enlargement of the eyelid the design of this curved staff is clearly distinguishable surrounded by four letters."[38]

There are four Greek letters visible on the coin: **Y CAI** - part of the inscription, Father Filas speculated:

"TIBERIO[Y CAI]SAROS"

"of Tiberius Caesar." In English lettering this would be written

"TIBERIO[U CAI]SAROS"

Above: Ancient pollen taken from the shroud by Professor Max Frei. Right: Fr. Francis Filas, S.J. discovered Pilate's coins that were placed on the eyelids of Christ and are visible on the Shroud — both recording the age of the shroud to be almost 2,000 years old.

the *OU* and the *OS* being the genitive endings "of Tiberius Caesar." But he had a problem - a mistake in spelling. The Latin C is used rather than the Greek *K (kappa)*. It should read *Y KAI* not *Y CAI*.

Suprisingly, Father Filas's discovery caused consternation within STURP, and Samuel Pellicori, a physicist at the research Center of Santa Barbara, the spokesman for the group, claimed the "discovery" was the fruit of Father Filas's imagination. "In fact the spotted nature of the image enables the mind to connect dots and to find letters all over. You can find the initials of your own name if you look hard enough."[39] But this is just not true. The *Y CAI* is clearly visible in the photographic enlargement for anyone who has eyes to see. I find it hard to believe, that when Father Filas read his paper to the STURP conference at Los Alamos in 1979, he was received in almost the same way as Yves Delage was by the French Academy of Science in 1902. Father Filas described the scene in a letter to Brother Eymard:

"Father Filas replied to me with an admirable letter dated 20 December 1981. We owe it to his memory to quote it at length. He begins by telling me how he delivered his first communication to Los Alamos in October 1979, encountering 'from at least half the group icy silence, of resentment, hostility and almost derision. Their attitude was so flagrantly non-scientific and unobjective, that I received at least half a dozen letters after this meeting from other members of STURP apologizing for the discourteous treatment which had met my boldness in daring to suggest to this group that I knew something which they, the group, did not know.'

"There may indeed be something in that: jealousy and resentment against the Catholic religious, whose scientific formation in mathematics and chemistry, allied to a doctorate in theology, did not prevent 'certain members of STURP and other critics from treating me,' he wrote, 'as some sort of clerical illiterate.'

"STURP appears unanimous in its opposition to the coins, whereas Heller, I am able to state, regards Father Filas's work to be very serious - but only in private conversation.[Heller had also remained silent at the New London Symposium when asked if the Shroud was authentic.] Jackson, Jumper and Stevenson are today strangely silent on the subject, after having anticipated the find themselves."[40]

Again this is just bad science. Is biblical archaeology not a reputable science, or do only physics and chemistry qualify for this title?

Unlike other photographs, the Shroud contains a three-dimensional "code." From density scans, by a VP-8 Image analyzer a three dimensional image can be constructed, which is impossible with any other photograph.

"Besides, how could Pellicori state that I was taking my desires for reality by saying I wanted to see a coin of Pilate when I am not a numismatist and before tumbling accidentally on this I could not have distinguished a Pilate coin from a hole in the wall. I first had to visit a local numismatist who pointed out to me the books to consult. It was only then that I exclaimed EUREKA on discovering that it all coincided with Pilate's lepton. Then came the discovery of not only ONE, but TWO coins of Pilate with spelling mistakes."[41]

Father Filas's discovery has happily been confirmed by the two American scientists we saw above in connection with the Sudarium of Oviedo, Dr. Alan and Mrs. Mary Whanger, who picked up the research on the Shroud where STURP had left off. Dr. Whanger in 1981 had developed a new method of photographic analysis which he called "polarized image overlay technique. "When two superimposed images are simultaneously projected on to a screen through polarizing filters, a third filter will allow close-up comparison of details. So clearly did the coins on the eyes of Our Lord appear, that today no one, including STURP, doubts them.

"Using the polarized image technique with a photograph of Filas's coin and a computer enhanced photograph of the area over the right eye...from the Enrie 1931 photograph, we found that there is nearly a perfect match between these two images...There are at least 74 points of congruence with all the letters UCAI. [It only takes '45 to 60 points to establish the identity or same source of face images' in a court of law.]

"...The image of a coin over the left eye is less distinct than that over the right eye, but by using the polarized image overlay technique

to compare with various coins we were able to identify that coin as well. Interestingly, this image coincides with another Pontius Pilate lepton, the so-called Julia lepton, struck only in A.D. 29. We counted 73 points of congruence between this image and the coin.[42]

This particular coin, the lepton, the smallest coin in circulation at the time, is the "widow's mite" of the Gospel. One can easily speculate that it was Our Blessed Lady herself, who placed these two "widow's mites" on the eyes of her dead Son. "And he said: 'Verily I say unto you, that this poor widow hath cast in more than they all: For all these have of their abundance cast into the offerings of God: but she of her want, hath cast in all the living she had" (Luke 21:3,4). This incident took place in Tuesday of Holy Week, and surely Our Lord had Our Lady in mind when He spoke these words. So what at first might seem to be a superstitious practice, becomes instead a beautiful parable of Our Lady, putting the whole of her substance, her beloved Son, into the treasury of God's love.

The Whangers have also contributed additional "new evidence" which again rebuts the claims of the Carbon-14 daters, and also in the process, exonerating, like Father Filas, another much maligned Shroud researcher, Max Frei. Frei, a Swiss criminologist and botanist, had tried to prove after studying the pollen on the Shroud, that it originated in the Holy Land, not in Europe as the Carbon-14 daters claimed. Here again are the Whangers presenting more results of their study of the Shroud by the use of their new photographic technique:

"On the Shroud of Turin are images of large numbers of flowers and plants...A number of these images, which may include not only flowers, but in some cases also buds, leaves, stems, and fruit, can be recognized by comparing them with botanical drawings. We feel we have made tentative identification of 28 of these plants, which we have photographed in detail. Of these, all 28 grow in Israel either in Jerusalem itself or in the nearby desert or Dead Sea areas. Using material taken from the Shroud on sticky tapes pressed into its surface which picked up hundreds of pollens, Dr. Max Frei was able to identify at least 58 different pollens on the Shroud. He had already identified pollens from 25 of the 28 plants whose images we have identi-

fied, with some variability in a few of the species...

"These flower images on the Shroud were obviously much more visible in the earlier centuries of the Shroud's existence, since they have been accurately copied in a number of early iconographic and other artistic depictions of Christ in many media including Byzantine coins between the 3rd and 10th centuries. These observable data on the flower images and the pollens from the Shroud in addition to vast information from other sources indicate that the conclusion of the carbon dating studies of 1988 that the Shroud is of medieval origin (i.e.,13th or 14th century) is anomalous and erroneous, and that the Shroud's origin is Israel in the first century."[43]

This wonderful research of the Whangers has been confirmed from a surprising source:

"JERUSALEM - Images of flower and pollen samples that appear on the Shroud of Turin are those of plant species that grow in the area of Jerusalem, says an Israeli botanist. "The assemblage of plants...shows (the Shroud) could only come from the Middle East, and the best fit is Jerusalem," said Hebrew University Professor Avinoam Danin, an expert on the flora of the Holy Land. Some 96% of the 28 flower species identified on the Shroud grow between Jerusalem and the Qumran Caves. Add the southern Dead Sea area to the equation and 100% of the species can found, said Danin."[44]

Is it not beautiful to imagine Mary Magdalen, Mary Cleophas, and the other holy women, picking an abundance of flowers, and banking them around the dead body of Our Lord before it was covered with the Shroud?

Finally let me conclude with a moving exhortation of Pope Pius XI given in 1936 to a group of pilgrims just after he had given them pictures of the Face of Our Lord on the Holy Shroud:

"These pictures of her Divine Son, and we may perhaps say the most thought-provoking, the most beautiful, the most precious that one can imagine. They come precisely from that object which still remains mysterious, but which has certainly not been made with human hands (one may say that this is now proved), that is the Holy Shroud of Turin. We have used the word mysterious, because that holy thing is still surrounded by considerable mystery; but it is certainly something more sacred than anything else; and indeed (one can

henceforth say that the geniuses of it is proved in the most positive way, even when setting aside all ideas of faith or Christian piety), it is not a human work."[45]

In the face of such a "mystery" as that of the Holy Shroud, one can only say in the words of Doctor Barbet, "What is poor science but ignorance disguised!"[46]

****

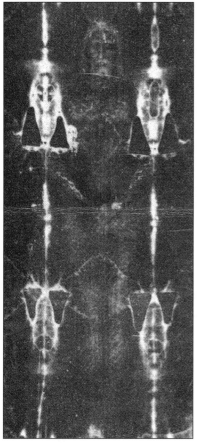 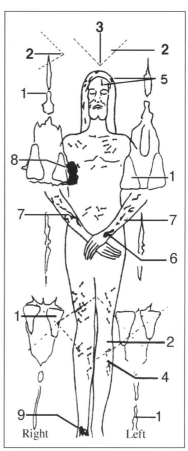

1. Scorchings and patches
2. Water
3. Full body
4. Scourges
5. Thorns

6. Nail (wrist)
7. Blood
8. Spear thrust
9. Nails (feet)

References

1. Fr. Werner Bulst, S.J., *The Shroud of Turin*, translated by Fr. Stephen McKenna, C.S.S.R. and Fr. James J. Galvin, C.S.S.R., Bruce Publishing Co., 1965, pp. 82-101.
2. Bro. Bruno Bonnet-Eymard, "The Holy Shroud Tested by Science, Science Tested by the Holy Shroud," *The Catholic Counter-Reformation*, September 1984, Morden, Surrey, England, pp. 4, 5.

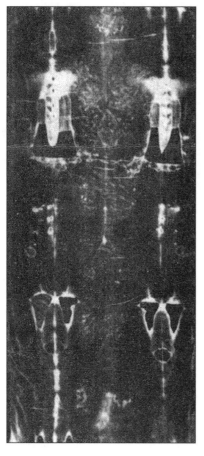 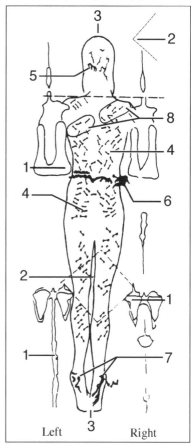

1. Scorchings and patches
2. Water
3. Full body
4. Scourges
5. Thorns

6. Blood from cava vein after body was taken down from the Cross
7. Nails (feet)
8. Crossbeam (*patibulum*)

3. In these days when so many "Catholic" scholars deny or cast doubt on the bodily Resurrection of Our Lord, it is good to recall one of the qualities of the glorified body which concerns us here, namely, its brightness or clarity:

"The next quality is brightness, *by which the bodies of the Saints shall shine like the sun, according to the words of Our Lord recorded in the Gospel of St. Matthew: 'The just shall shine as the sun, in the kingdom of their Father' (Matt. 13:43). To remove the possibility of doubt on the subject, He exemplifies this in His Transfiguration. This quality the Apostle sometimes calls* glory, *sometimes* brightness: *'He will reform the body of his glory' (1Cor. 15:43). Of this glory the Israelites beheld some image in the desert, when the face of Moses, after he had enjoyed the presence and conversation of God, shone with such luster that they could not look on it. The brightness is a sort of radiance reflected on the body from the supreme happiness of the soul. It is a participation in that bliss which the soul enjoys, just as the soul itself is rendered happy by participation in the happiness of God. Unlike the gift of impassability, this quality is not common to all in the same degree. All the bodies of the Saints will be equally impassible; but the brightness of all will not be the same, for according to the Apostle, 'One is the glory of the sun, another the glory of the stars, for star differeth from star in glory; so also is the resurrection of the dead' (1Cor. 15:41, 42)."*

Catechism of the Council of Trent, Doubleday and Co., Garden City, NY, 1978, pp. 97-100.

4. Ian Wilson, *The Shroud of Turin,* Doubleday and Co., Garden City, NY, 1978, pp. 97-100.

5. Council for the Study of the Shroud, P.O. Box 52327, Durham, NC, 27717. Internet: http:/dmi-www.mc.../shroud/sudarium.

6. Thomas Heaphy, *The Likeness of Christ,* edited by Wyke Bayliss, F.S.A., Society for Promoting Christian Knowledge, London, 1886, pp.51, 52.

7. Dorothy Scallan, *The Holy Man of Tours,* edited by Fr. Emeric B. Scallan, S.T.B., Tan Books and Publishers, 1990, Rockford, IL, pp. 128, 129.

8. Scallan , *op. cit.,* pp. 145, 146.

9. Since the "miracle of The Vatican" the Popes have authorized printed copies of the Veil of Veronica, requiring that they be made on linen or silk. They are exactly the kind possessed by Monsieur Dupont, touched to the Wood of the True Cross, the Sacred Lance, and the authentic Veil of Veronica, and sealed with a Cardinal's seal in witness of this fact. They are available

from many Carmels throughout the country associated with the Arch Confraternity of the Holy Face.

10. Fr. André Feuillet, "The Identification and Disposition of the Funerary Linens of Jesus' Burial According to the Data of the Fourth Gospel," *Shroud Spectrum International*, Indiana Center for Shroud Studies, Nashville, IN, 1982.
11. Wilson, *op. cit.*, p. 14.
12. Bulst, *op. cit.*, p. 110.
13. Wilson, p. 20.
14. Pierre Barbet, M.D., *A Doctor at Calvary*, translated by the Earl of Wicklow, Doubleday and Co., New York, 1963, pp. 6, 7.
15. Barbet, *op. cit.*, pp. 8, 9.
16. Bulst, pp. 109, 110.
17. Barbet, pp. 140, 141.
18. Barbet, p. 1.
19. Barbet, pp. 29, 30.
20. *L'Osservatore Romano*, January 31, 1938.
21. Fr. Austin Flannery, O.P., Editor, *Vatican Council II*, The Liturgical Press, Collegeville, MN, 1975, p. 962.
22. F. De Grandmaison, M.D., *Twenty Cures at Lourdes: Medically Discussed*, translated by Dom Hugo Bevenot, O.S.B. and Dom Luke Izard, O.S.B., Herder Book Co., St. Louis, 1912, p. 264.
23. Farley Clinton, "The Problems of the Shroud," *The Wanderer*, November 3, 1988, p. 6.
24. Group Captain, G.L. Cheshire, *Pilgrimage to the Shroud*, McGraw Hill Book Co., New York, 1956, p. 63.
25. Clinton, *op. cit.*, p. 6.
26. Fr. Peter Rinaldi, S.D.B., *It Is the Lord*, Warner Books, New York, 1973, p. 111.
27. Bro. Bruno Bonnet-Eymard, "The Holy Shroud Tested by Science, Science Tested by the Holy Shroud," *The Catholic Counter-Reformation*, Morden, Surrey, England, September 1984, p. 6.
28. Barbet, p. 18.
29. John H. Heller, *Report on the Shroud of Turin*, Houghton Mifflin, Boston, 1983, quoted in Eymard, *op. cit.*, p. 15.
30. Eymard, p.21. To Heller's credit, it must be said that he later

honestly summarized this disgraceful incident in almost the identical words of Yves Delage:

"It is certainly true that if a similar number of data had been found in the funerary linen attributed to Alexander the Great, Genghis Khan or Socrates, there would be no doubt in anyone's mind that it was indeed the shroud of that historical person. But because of the unique position that Jesus holds, such evidence is not enough." Heller, *op. cit.*, cited in Eymard, *op. cit.*, p. 15.

31. Kenneth E. Stevenson and Gary R. Habermas, *The Shroud and the Controversy*, Thomas Nelson Publishers, Nashville, TN, 990, p. 97.

32. D. Collins, *The Human Revolution*, the Phaidon Press, p. 51, quoted in M. Bowden, *Ape-Man Fact or Fallacy*, Sovereign Publications, Bromley Kent, 1977, p. 55.

"Not all of the twenty-two scientists who participated in the 1986 Congress in Turin which planned the Carbon-14 testing, accepted the results. For example, the American archaeologist, William Meacham, who uses Carbon-14 regularly in his field work said:

'The lab work on the Shroud was very sophisticated but the planning and sampling methodology was very shabby,' Mr. Meacham said. *"Carbon-14 (C-14) tests conducted independently at three separate laboratories were questionable because all three labs used identical samples,"* he said. *"The samples were taken from a repaired corner which had been scorched in a fire in 1532. The C-14 date may reflect the influence of the 1532 fire rather than the actual age of the linen."'*

"Testing on Shroud Flawed: Scientist," *Courier-Mail*, Brisbane, Australia, 15 October, 1988. Cf. also Stevenson, Op. cit., pp. 184-186.

33. *The Tablet*, London, October 15, 1988.

34. Stephano M. Paci, "The Case Is Not Closed!" *30 Days*, June 1990, pp. 80-106.

Brother Bruno's circumstantial case against the Carbon-14 test is very compelling. Dr. Michael Tite of the British Museum, for some unexplained reason, was placed in charge of the testing. He knew that the Catholic Modernists, Canon Ulysses Chevalier and Fr. Herbert Thurston, claimed that the Shroud was a medieval forgery dating from the 13th or 14th century. Tite, on his own admission, asked Jacques Evin, a French archaeologist, to find *"a medieval control sample, which is as similar as possible in terms of weave and colours as the Shroud...which dates from the 13th or 14th century A.D., preferably the latter."* Jacques Evin found a cloth that matched

Tite's specifications: it was the herringbone patterned cope of the Franciscan, St. Louis d'Anjou, called by the Spaniards, St. Louis Obispo, who became a bishop in 1296. Evin and a confederate entered the Church of St. Maximin, where the cope is kept, and without notifying the parish priest, snipped a sample. Inexplicably the pieces of cloth cut from the Shroud in Turin were of a different size and weight when they arrived at the testing laboratories. Brother Bruno believes that Tite substituted the sample from the cope of St. Louis for that of the Shroud.

There are many more incriminating details, but they would take too long to develop here. The clincher is that Tite's superior, Dr. Edward Hall, who called the marks on the Shroud "pig's blood," was given a gift of a million pounds by forty-five "rich friends" for having "determined last year that the Shroud of Turin was a medieval fake." (See *Daily Telegraph* March 24, 1989, Good Friday.) Hall announced that he was retiring, and that he would use the money to create a new chair of archaeology at Oxford to be filled by his friend Dr. Michael Tite! Just look at the photograph taken of these two men at the time they were announcing that the Shroud was a fake. It speaks more than words.

Bro. Bruno Bonnet-Eymard's two volume work in French has not yet been translated into English, but his case is also presented in a series of articles in the English edition (Morden, Surrey, England) of *Catholic Counter-Reformation*, running from December 1979 through March of 1996. These articles have been summarized by Mark Fellows in *The Remnant* for August 31, 1996. Mark Fellows' excellent series of articles on the Shroud entitled *A Second Coming*, has been published in booklet form by The Remnant Bookstore, St. Paul, MN, 55117.

35. Heller, *op. cit.*, quoted in Eymard, p. 15.

36. A.P. Bender, "Beliefs, Rites and Customs of the Jews Connected with Death, Burial and Mourning," Part IV *Jewish Quarterly Review* VII, 1895; cited in Wilson, op. cit., p. 200.

37. Bro. Bruno Bonnet-Eymard, "Threats Over the Holy Shroud," *The Catholic Counter-Reformation*, August-September, 1986, Morden, Surrey, England, p 26.

38. Eymard, *op. cit.*, p. 26.

39. Eymard, p. 26.

40. Eymard, p. 27.

41. Eymard, p. 27.

42. Alan D. Whanger and Mary Whanger, "Polarized image over-

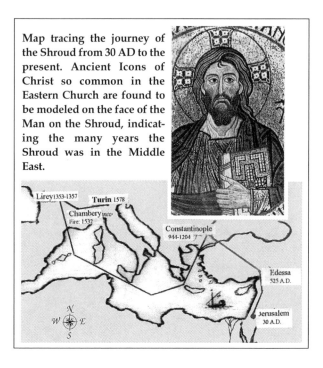

Map tracing the journey of the Shroud from 30 AD to the present. Ancient Icons of Christ so common in the Eastern Church are found to be modeled on the face of the Man on the Shroud, indicating the many years the Shroud was in the Middle East.

lay technique: a new image comparison method and its applications," *Applied Optics*, Vol. 24, No. 6, 15 March 1985.

43. Dr. Alan and Mrs Mary Whanger, *Floral, Coin, and Other Non-Body Images on the Shroud of Turin*, Duke University, Durham, NC, 27710, U.S.A.

44. *The Tablet*, Brooklyn, NY, August 18, 1997.

45. *L'Osservatore Romano*, September 7, 8, 1936; quoted in Barbet, pp. 10, 11.

46. Barbet, p. 87.

"I don't think a lot of people realize the significance of what we're [STURP team] dealing with. People say, 'Well, that's nice,' which is characteristic of the attitude of our times. But if you assume that this is Christ; and this body left the cloth without any indication of decay; and whatever happened to this body that caused it to leave a photographic negative on the cloth: well, what we're dealing with here quite simply is Christ's promise of eternal life."

ADDENDUM

The Internet has become an invaluable tool for scholars engaged in research. There is now a new Web Site dedicated exclusively to the Holy Shroud, http://www.shroud.com, which was opened 18 months ago by Barrie Schwortz, former STURP member, whom we have seen above. It has already been accessed an amazing 86,000 times.[1] But as valuable as the Internet is, there is still no substitute for a book, and it was a real event when the long awaited *The Shroud of Turin: An Adventure of Discovery*, by Dr. Alan and Mrs. Mary Whanger,[2] presenting their twenty-one years of research on the Shroud, finally came out this Spring.

The Whangers emphasize that as the linen of the Shroud ages, it becomes yellowish, the same color as the images it contains, making them more and more difficult to see, and it is just a matter of time before they are gone altogether, doubtless a punishment on our unbelieving world. In early paintings of the Shroud the flowers, which are now almost invisible, were clearly delineated and were copied even on small coins. The Whangers, through the use of their Polarized Image Overlay Technique, have been able to recover these images of the flowers which were buried with Jesus. The Whangers also noticed that during the Middle Ages, after the Shroud had been exhibited in France, there was a flurry of paintings depicting the instruments of the Passion, the nails, the lance, etc., but also what appeared to be small brush brooms. Mary Whanger writes:

"One day Alan asked me to come an look at a small area near the edge of the Shroud...and see if I could discern anything there. This was another of those occasions when he did not tell me what he had found, but wanted to see if I could find it, too. I studied the area for a

All that remains of the *Titulus of the Cross* kept in the Holy Cross Church in Rome.

few minutes, and then said, 'Well I see something that looks like a spoon.' 'What?!,' was his startled response. This was not what he had expected me to say. What he had seen was a small rectangular area which he thought might be a shallow box. We had seen such boxes in drawings of first century artifacts. The lifeblood was so valued by the Jews that any blood of a dead person that had been spilled, even blood spilled on the ground, would be carefully collected and placed in the tomb with the body. Since blood had obviously been spilled during the crucifixion, we thought it might be likely that a box containing bloody dirt had been placed in the tomb with the body. On closer examination, we saw that the bowl of the spoon or trowel is resting in the small box, and the handle extends below it. There is a dark spot in the box just at the edge of the bowl of the spoon which we speculate might be a lump of bloody dirt. And we feel we can distinguish a narrow strip of cloth that has been tied across the box to hold the spoon in position...Both the box with the cloth tie and the spoon or trowel are similar to such objects we found in photographs of first-century artifacts.

"Continuing to look for unusual patterns, Alan noticed a cone-shaped light area which then gave way to a group of irregular twisted lines that seemed to be coming out of the light area. We think that these might be images of twigs or stems bound together which extended out into finer bristles, such as might be found in a brush broom. There seem to be images of two of them, each about seventeen inches long. If this is correct, they would have been used to sweep up some of the blood that had fallen on the ground."[3]

Of course these beautiful Jewish funeral practices in reverence of the lifeblood, are meant to be a prophecy of the Most Precious Blood, since the lifeblood of Jesus becomes our lifeblood in the Blessed Eucharist.

The Whangers have also discovered on the Shroud the image of the "title," about which Pilate said: "What I have

108

written, I have written" (John 19:22). But let me give a little background so we can appreciate the significance of this most important discovery. This title is found in all four Gospels: "THIS IS JESUS THE KING OF THE JEWS" (Matthew 27:37), "THE KING OF THE JEWS" (Mark 15:26), "THIS IS THE KING OF THE JEWS" (Luke 23:28), and "JESUS OF NAZARETH, THE KING OF THE JEWS" (John 19:19). The title is substantially the same in all four Gospels, but John, who stood at the foot of the Cross with the Mother of Jesus, must have been the most literal. He is the only one who uses the term "OF NAZARETH." This title was found in Jerusalem by St. Helena, the mother of Constantine, at the same time when she found the True Cross. It is now kept in Rome in the Church of the Holy Cross. Unfortunately it has greatly deteriorated over the centuries, and all that remains are the words "OF NAZARETH" in Latin and Greek, written backwards as in Hebrew. It as if the Holy Spirit had deliberately preserved this phrase as a witness for our unbelieving generation to the historicity of the Gospel of St. John.

There is a movement underway today by certain Jewish pressure groups like the Anti-Defamation League of B'nai B'rith, the American Jewish Congress, etc., in collaboration of many Modernist Catholic priests, who do not believe in the historicity of the Gospel of St. John, to force on the Church the lie that Christianity, beginning with the Gospel of St. John, is the origin of Anti-Semitism, which culminated in the Nazi Holocaust. Cardinal Bernadine of Chicago repeated this calumny in Jerusalem shortly before

The Cathedral at Turin, sanctuary of the Holy Shroud.

his death, to the great applause of the liberal media, both secular and Catholic. During Holy Week of last year there appeared on French television, but it could just as easily been American television, a five hour documentary series entitled *Corpus Christi*, presenting this big lie by a panel of 27 "experts," mostly Jews and Catholic priests. During the course of this series one of the Catholic priests, Father Puech, made the incredible remark: "I cannot say whether this relic [the title] is prior to the late Byzantine period, 5th-7th century; or rather the Middle Ages when the Shroud of Turin was fabricated. About the 13th or 14th century..."[4]

So much for background. Here again is Mary Whanger:

"Alan made a slide photograph of the replica [the title] in Rome to use with our Polarized Image Overlay Technique for comparison studies with the faint images on the Shroud. With rising excitement we could see that the letters whose images are on the Shroud have the same configuration and relation to each other as a A, a Z, and a rounded E on the replica. The replica, then gave us an idea of what the other letters might be on the Shroud and served as a template for comparison studies. We were eventually able to discern, in three separate lines, parts of several of the Greek letters, several Latin letters, and possible fragments of two or three of the Aramaic or Hebrew letters whose images are on the Shroud."[5]

The letters the Whangers discovered on the Shroud, Providentially, are from the phrase "OF NAZARETH," thus confirming in one fell swoop, the authenticity of the title, the authenticity of the Shroud, and the historicity of the Gospel of St. John!

References

1. Marinelli, Emanuella, "Shadow Letters on the Shroud," *Inside the Vatican*, December, 1997, p. 56.

2. Whanger, Mary and Alan, *The Shroud of Turin, An Adventure of Discovery*, Providence House Publishers, Franklin, Tennessee, 1998.

3. Whanger, *op. cit.*, p. 94.

4. Bonnet-Eymard, Brother Bruno, "The Truth of the Gospels, a Reply to Arte's 'Twenty-Seven,'" *The Catholic Counter-Reformation in the XXth Century*, Shawinigan, Que., Canada, August 1997, p. 18.

5. Whanger, p. 99.

Further Information from the Publishers

The Franciscan Friars of the Immaculate, publishers of *St. Thérèse, Doctor of the Little Way, A Handbook on Guadalupe* and other books on the Eucharist and Our Lady, walk in the footsteps of St. Maximilian Kolbe, the hero of Auschwitz. They concentrate their efforts in the mass media to further the reign of the Sacred Heart of Jesus through total consecration to Mary Immaculate.

The Academy of the Immaculate, a non-profit Roman Catholic organization for the promotion of the theological studies of the Immaculate Virgin, works in collaboration with the Franciscan Friars of the Immaculate. Some of the recent publications of the Friars and the Academy are:

All Generations Shall Call Me Blessed: *A Biblical Mariology* by Fr. Stefano Manelli, F.I. 393 pp. (19.95)

Totus Tuus: *Pope John Paul II's Program of Marian Consecration and Entrustment* by Msgr. Arthur Calkins 334 pp. (14.95).

For the Life of the World: *St. Maximilian Kolbe and the Eucharist* by Fr. Jerzy Domanski, O.F.M. Conv. 160 pp. (8.95)

Jesus, Our Eucharistic Love: *Eucharistic Life As Exemplified by the Saints* by Fr. Stephano Manelli, F.I. 118 pp. (5.00)

A Handbook on Guadalupe: *A Comprehensive Coverage of Guadalupe* Edited by a Friar of the Immaculate 240 pp. (12.50)

St. Thérèse, Doctor of the Little Way: *A compilation of the past and latest on the New Doctor of the Church* Edited by a Friar of the Immaculate, 180 pp (9.50).

Virgo Facta Ecclesia – St. Francis of Assisi and His Charism: *A brief biography on the Saint with reflections on his charism for our times* by the Franciscans of the Immaculate. (5.00)

When ordering these books please include along with your payment, postage and handling as follows:

In the USA and Canada: $2.00 for the first book, 75¢ for each additional book.

Other countries: $5.00 for first book, $1.00 for each additional book.

For multiple copies & special rates for parishes and religious organizations, write:

Academy of the Immaculate, POB 667, Valatie, NY 12184

Or phone/FAX (518) 758-1584, E-mail - mimike@pipeline.com

For quotations on attractive bulk rates, shipped directly from the printery contact: Friars of the Immaculate,
(508) 984-1856, FAX (508) 996-8296, E-mail - ffi@ici.net.

Park Press, Inc. – P.O. Box 475, 355 6th Ave. N., Waite Park, MN 56387